Blue Flame Favorites

A COLLECTION OF FAVORITE
OKLAHOMA NATURAL GAS RECIPES
COMPILED OVER 70 YEARS

Blue Flame Favorites

A COLLECTION OF FAVORITE OKLAHOMA NATURAL GAS RECIPES COMPILED OVER 70 YEARS

Oklahoma Natural Gas Company
P.O. Box 401
Oklahoma City, Oklahoma 73101-0401
Telephone: 405-530-2532

ISBN: 0-9721342-0-4

Edited, Designed, and Manufactured by
Favorite Recipes® Press
An imprint of

FRP

P.O. Box 305142
Nashville, Tennessee 37230
(800) 358-0560

Art Director: Steve Newman
Book Designer: Jim Scott
Project Editor: Georgia Brazil

Manufactured in the United States of America
First Printing: 2003
7,500 copies
Second Printing: 2004
3,000 copies

Contents

Preface

For nearly 100 years, Oklahoma Natural Gas Company has delivered the natural gas that has kept our customers warm, their water hot, and their clothes dry.

And for many of those years, gas cooking and good recipes have also been synonymous with ONG. Providing recipes, cooking tips, and conservation information has been at the core of our relationship with customers. And it is to celebrate that relationship that we decided to produce this cookbook.

But we're more than just recipes. Our company was born on the eve of statehood in the heart of a vast energy resource. We are proud to play a leading role in both the physical infrastructure and the social fabric of Oklahoma through the delivery of reliable natural gas service. We have grown as the state has grown—vigorous, viable, and proud. Giving to the communities we live in and the customers we serve is an integral part of our history. Our community investment program doesn't stop with dollars, either. ONG employees give valuable time and contribute their diverse talents to a host of organizations that make our state a better place to live.

It is only fitting, then, that the proceeds from the sale of "Blue Flame Favorites" will be given to local charities. So, we hope these recipes will fill your home with the aroma of good food, the warmth of fond memories, and the satisfaction of helping others. And on behalf of Oklahoma Natural Gas Company, thank you for being a part of our extended family.

Samuel Combs III
President, Oklahoma Natural Gas Company

Foreword

"Blue Flame Favorites" is a collection of recipes enjoyed by our customers over the past 70 years, thanks to the efforts and expertise of Oklahoma Natural Gas Home Economists, who lovingly tested recipes year after year so that these delicious dishes could be shared with our "ONG family."

The recipes we chose for our cookbook reflect the richness of the various cultures and cuisines of Oklahomans as experienced by our parents, grandparents, and even great-grandparents. For that reason, the recipes read like a history book, evoking the spirit of our state.

The selected recipes are favorites that were tested for demonstrations, seasonal recipe sheets, and customer newsletters. In addition to ingredients, you'll find some history intertwined to briefly describe life from the inception of Oklahoma Natural Gas to the present.

We hope you enjoy reading "Blue Flame Favorites" and once again trying some of our favorite recipes.

The Editors

The first practical use of natural gas in the late 1700s was for
public street lighting. Streets at night took on a warm, friendly glow.

Appetizers and Beverages

Avocado Rolls

1 cup mashed avocado
8 ounces cream cheese, softened
1/2 cup (2 ounces) shredded Cheddar cheese
2 teaspoons lime juice
1/2 teaspoon Worcestershire sauce

1 to 2 drops hot red pepper sauce
1 garlic clove, crushed
1/2 teaspoon salt
1 1/4 cups finely chopped cashews
Paprika to taste

Combine the avocado, cream cheese and Cheddar cheese in a bowl and mix well. Add the lime juice, Worcestershire sauce, hot red pepper sauce, garlic and salt and mix well. Add the cashews and mix well. Chill, covered, for 30 minutes.

Divide the mixture into equal portions and shape each half into a 1 1/2-inch thick cylinder. Roll each cylinder in paprika to coat. Chill, wrapped in plastic, for 2 hours or longer. Serve sliced with crackers.

Yield: 2 1/2 cups

Cheese Straws

2 (1-pound) loaves sliced white bread
2 (5-ounce) jars sharp cheese spread, softened
1 cup (2 sticks) margarine, softened
1/2 teaspoon hot red pepper sauce

1 teaspoon Worcestershire sauce
1/2 teaspoon onion powder
1 teaspoon dillweed
1 teaspoon Beau Monde seasoning
Dash of cayenne pepper

Remove the crusts from the bread and slice the bread into finger-size slices. Combine the cheese spread, margarine, hot red pepper sauce and Worcestershire sauce in a bowl until fluffy. Add the onion powder, dillweed, Beau Monde seasoning and cayenne pepper and mix well.

Spread the cheese mixture thinly on the tops and sides of the bread slices. Place the slices on a lightly greased baking sheet, cover with plastic wrap and freeze.

Preheat the gas oven to 350 degrees. Place the frozen straws on a greased baking sheet. Bake for 12 to 15 minutes or until brown.

Yield: 3 dozen straws

Olive Cheese Nuggets

1 cup (4 ounces) shredded sharp Cheddar cheese
1/4 cup (1/2 stick) margarine, softened
3/4 cup sifted flour
1/8 teaspoon salt
1/2 teaspoon paprika
1/4 teaspoon cayenne pepper (optional)
35 to 40 stuffed green olives

Preheat the gas oven to 400 degrees. Combine the cheese and margarine in a bowl and mix well. Sift the flour, salt, paprika and cayenne pepper together, add to the cheese mixture and mix until a dough forms. Knead on a floured surface if necessary.

Shape approximately 1 teaspoon of dough around each olive to enclose and seal completely. Place the olives on an ungreased baking sheet. Bake for 12 to 15 minutes or until golden brown. Serve warm or cold.

The unbaked olives may be frozen and baked as needed. The cheese dough may be shaped into pencil-size sticks and baked as above to make crisp delicious Cheese Sticks.

Yield: 12 servings

In 1905, the Glenn Pool oil field was discovered east of Sapulpa in the Creek Nation of Indian Territory. This was the beginning of the discovery of natural resources that would change the state forever. After the discovery of natural gas, early entrepreneurs made wholesale contracts to switch customers from manufactured to natural gas. A 20-year charter was granted to these entrepreneurs under the laws of the Oklahoma Territory and this was the beginning of Oklahoma Natural Gas Company.

Manhattan Meatballs

2/3 recipe (2 packages) frozen Make-Ahead Meatballs (below)
1 (10-ounce) jar apricot preserves
1/2 cup barbecue sauce

Preheat the gas oven to 350 degrees. Place the meatballs in a lightly greased baking dish.

Combine the preserves and barbecue sauce in a bowl and mix well. Pour the mixture over the meatballs. Bake for 45 to 50 minutes for frozen meatballs or 30 minutes for thawed meatballs.

Meatballs with sauce may be wrapped in plastic wrap and frozen. Add about 5 minutes to the baking time.

Yield: 10 to 12 servings

Make-Ahead Meatballs

2 pounds ground beef
1 pound bulk pork sausage
3 cups soft bread crumbs
3 eggs, beaten
1/2 cup milk

1 1/2 teaspoons Worcestershire sauce
1/2 cup instant minced onion
3 tablespoons chopped parsley
1 tablespoon salt
1/2 teaspoon pepper

Preheat the gas oven to 350 degrees. Combine the ground beef, bulk pork sausage, bread crumbs, eggs, milk and Worcestershire sauce in a bowl and mix well. Add the instant minced onion, parsley, salt and pepper and mix well.

Shape the meat mixture into 1-inch balls and place in an ungreased baking dish. Bake for 30 minutes or until cooked through; drain. Cool for 5 minutes. Freeze, uncovered, for 15 minutes.

Divide the partially frozen meatballs into 3 portions and place each portion in a freezer container. Label and date containers and store in the freezer.

Spiced Nuts

1/4 cup water
1 cup sugar
1/2 teaspoon ground cloves
1/2 teaspoon nutmeg

2 teaspoons cinnamon
1/4 teaspoon salt
2 cups mixed salted nuts

Combine the water, sugar, ground cloves, nutmeg, cinnamon and salt in a small saucepan and mix well. Cook over a medium flame until the sugar dissolves, stirring constantly. Cook, uncovered, to 234 to 240 degrees on a candy thermometer, soft-ball stage. Remove the mixture from the flame. Add the nuts and stir to coat well. Spread the nuts on waxed paper, separate with a fork and cool completely.

Yield: 2 cups

Onion Toasted Walnuts

2 cups shelled walnuts
2 tablespoons margarine, melted

1 to 2 tablespoons onion soup mix

Preheat the gas oven to 325 degrees. Combine the walnuts and margarine in a bowl and mix to coat. Arrange in a shallow baking dish. Bake for 10 to 15 minutes or until golden brown. Sprinkle the soup mix over the walnuts and toss lightly. Spread on paper towels and cool completely.

Yield: 2 cups

Hot Artichoke Spread

1 (14-ounce) can artichoke hearts, drained, chopped

1 cup grated Parmesan cheese
1 cup mayonnaise or low-fat mayonnaise

Preheat the gas oven to 350 degrees. Combine the artichokes, Parmesan cheese and mayonnaise in a bowl and mix well. Spread the mixture in a greased pie plate. Bake for 30 minutes or until bubbly. Blot excess oil from surface with a paper towel if necessary. Serve with crackers or melba toast.

Yield: 2 cups

Pineapple Cheese Ball

16 ounces cream cheese, softened
2 teaspoons seasoned salt
2 tablespoons finely chopped green
   bell pepper

2 tablespoons finely chopped onion
1/4 cup crushed pineapple, drained
2 cups chopped pecans

Combine the cream cheese and seasoned salt in a mixing bowl and beat until smooth. Fold in the green pepper, onion, pineapple and half the pecans.

Shape the mixture into a ball and roll in the remaining pecans to coat. Chill for 2 to 4 hours. Serve with crackers and fresh fruit.

Yield: 2 cups

Creamy Dip for Fruit

8 ounces cream cheese, softened

1 (7-ounce) jar marshmallow creme

Combine the cream cheese and marshmallow creme in a mixing bowl and beat until fluffy. Serve with fresh fruit.

Yield: 2 cups

Energy Saver: *Leave the oven and broiler doors closed while foods are cooking.*

Layered Crab Dip

2 (6-ounce) cans crab meat, drained, flaked
2 green onions, minced
1/2 cup chopped cucumber
1/2 cup chopped red onion
1 medium tomato, finely chopped
2 tablespoons minced parsley
1/4 cup lime juice
1/4 cup lemon juice
Freshly ground pepper to taste
16 ounces low-fat cream cheese, softened
1/2 cup low-fat mayonnaise
1 (8-ounce) carton avocado dip

Combine the crab meat, green onions, cucumber, red onion, tomato and parsley in a large bowl and mix well. Pour the lime juice and lemon juice over the mixture and sprinkle with pepper. Chill, covered, for 6 hours or longer.

Combine the cream cheese and mayonnaise in a medium bowl and blend well. Spread the cream cheese mixture over a large serving platter and layer with the avocado dip.

Drain the crab meat mixture thoroughly and spoon over the avocado layer. Serve with crackers or tortilla chips.

Yield: 12 servings

In 1906, land was acquired for oil production and many wells were drilled during this period. In the 1920s ONG underwent various changes in ownership and control. It seemed growth would continue indefinitely . . . which it did for a few years. Then, on October 29, 1929, the stock market collapsed. Many people lost their jobs and were out of money. It was rumored that the company was going into receivership in 1931. There were frequent changes in leadership and the name changed to Oklahoma Natural Gas Corporation. The company survived and was reorganized and refinanced its debt. In 1934 the company incorporated and became the newly created Oklahoma Natural Gas Company and the old corporation was dissolved.

Baked Beef Dip

2 teaspoons margarine
1 cup chopped pecans
16 ounces cream cheese, softened
1 cup sour cream

1/4 cup milk
1/2 teaspoon garlic salt
2 (2 1/2-ounce) packages dried beef, chopped
4 teaspoons minced onion

Preheat the gas oven to 350 degrees. Melt the margarine in a saucepan or skillet over a medium flame. Add the pecans and cook until lightly browned, stirring occasionally. Drain and set the pecans aside.

Combine the cream cheese, sour cream, milk and garlic salt in a bowl and blend well. Fold in the dried beef and onion. Pour the mixture into a greased 1 1/2-quart baking dish and top with the pecans. Bake for 20 minutes or until heated through. Serve hot with crackers.

Yield: 4 cups

Creamy Dill Dip

1 cup sour cream
1 cup mayonnaise
1 1/2 teaspoons Worcestershire sauce
1 1/2 tablespoons instant minced onion

1 tablespoon parsley flakes
1 1/8 teaspoons Beau Monde seasoning
1 1/2 teaspoons dillweed

Combine the sour cream, mayonnaise and Worcestershire sauce in a bowl and blend well. Add the onion, parsley flakes, Beau Monde seaoning and dillweed and mix well. Chill, covered, for 2 hours or longer. Serve with chips or bite-size fresh vegetables.

Yield: 2 cups

Energy Saver: *Replace or clean the air filters in your forced air heating system at least twice a season.*

Oklahoma Caviar

1 (16-ounce) can black beans, drained
1 (8-ounce) can small kernel white corn, drained
1 (15-ounce) can diced tomatoes with green chiles
1 bunch green onions, chopped
1 yellow bell pepper, chopped
1 red bell pepper, chopped
1 green bell pepper, chopped
1 cup chopped fresh tomatoes
1 garlic clove, minced
1/4 cup chopped cilantro or parsley
1/4 cup red wine vinegar
3 tablespoons lemon juice
1/8 teaspoon cumin
Cayenne pepper to taste
Chili powder to taste
Garlic powder to taste

Combine the black beans, corn, tomatoes with green chiles, green onions, yellow, red and green peppers, fresh tomatoes, garlic and cilantro in a bowl. Add the red wine vinegar and lemon juice and toss to mix well. Sprinkle with cumin, cayenne pepper, chili powder and garlic powder and toss lightly. Chill, covered, for 4 hours or longer. Serve with tortilla chips, melba toast or toasted pita bread.

Yield: 12 servings

Spinach Dip

1 (10-ounce) package frozen chopped spinach, thawed
1 cup mayonnaise
1 cup sour cream
1 envelope vegetable soup mix
1 medium onion, chopped
1 (8-ounce) can water chestnuts, drained, chopped

Drain and squeeze dry the spinach. Combine the mayonnaise, sour cream and vegetable soup mix in a bowl and mix well. Add the spinach and mix well. Fold in the onion and water chestnuts. Chill, covered, for several hours or until serving time. Serve with crackers or bite-size fresh vegetables.

Yield: 3 cups

Hot Spiced Cider

6 cups apple juice
1/4 cup packed brown sugar

1/2 teaspoon whole cloves
3 inches cinnamon stick

Combine the apple juice and brown sugar in a saucepan and stir to mix well. Add the cloves and cinnamon. Simmer over a low flame for 20 to 30 minutes, stirring occasionally. Remove the cloves and cinnamon. Pour into mugs and serve with cinnamon sticks as stirrers if desired.

Yield: 10 to 12 servings

Mulled Tomato Juice

2 (46-ounce) cans tomato juice
1/2 cup (1 stick) margarine, melted
2 tablespoons Worcestershire sauce
10 drops hot red pepper sauce

1/4 teaspoon liquid smoke
1/2 teaspoon oregano
1 teaspoon celery salt

Combine the tomato juice, margarine, Worcestershire sauce, hot red pepper sauce and liquid smoke in a large saucepan and mix well. Add the oregano and celery salt and mix well. Bring to a boil, covered, over a medium flame. Reduce the flame and simmer for 10 to 15 minutes, stirring occasionally. Pour into mugs or serve chilled garnished with celery sticks.

Yield: 20 servings

Anniversary Fruit Punch

1 cup lemon juice
1 cup sugar
9 cups apple juice, chilled
4 1/2 cups orange juice, chilled

4 1/2 cups pineapple juice, chilled
1 orange, sliced
1 lemon, sliced

Combine the lemon juice and sugar in a large punch bowl and mix until the sugar dissolves. Add the apple juice, orange juice and pineapple juice and stir to mix well. Garnish with orange and lemon slices. Add ice cubes just before serving.

Yield: 20 servings

Key Lime Punch

1 pint lime sherbet, softened
1 (6-ounce) can frozen limeade concentrate, thawed

1 cup water
1 (28-ounce) bottle ginger ale, chilled

Combine the lime sherbet, limeade concentrate and water in a large punch bowl. Add the ginger ale gradually, stirring until slushy.

Yield: 10 servings

Pina Colada Flip

1 (46-ounce) can pineapple juice, chilled
1 (16-ounce) can cream of coconut

1 quart vanilla ice cream, softened
1 (28-ounce) bottle club soda, chilled

Combine the pineapple juice and cream of coconut in a punch bowl and mix well. Add the ice cream in spoonfuls. Pour the club soda slowly over the mixture, stirring gently.

Yield: 15 servings

Slushy Fruit Punch

3 envelopes unsweetened drink mix, any flavor
3 cups sugar
2 quarts water

Juice of 3 lemons
1 (46-ounce) can pineapple juice
3 bananas, mashed
1 (28-ounce) bottle lemon-lime soda

Combine the drink mix, sugar and water in a large container and mix well until the sugar dissolves. Add the lemon juice, pineapple juice, bananas and lemon-lime soda and mix well. Place in a covered container and freeze. Remove from the freezer 2 to 3 hours before serving. Let stand at room temperature, stirring occasionally until slushy.

Yield: 20 servings

The first pipeline laid by Oklahoma Natural Gas was a 12-inch 100-mile line laid from 10 miles south of Tulsa to Oklahoma City.

Soups and Salads

Black-Eyed Pea Soup

1 tablespoon olive oil
1 large onion, finely chopped
1 garlic clove, minced
1 (4-ounce) can chopped green chiles
4 (16-ounce) cans black-eyed peas, drained, rinsed
1 (10-ounce) can diced tomatoes with green chiles
3 (11-ounce) cans beef broth
1/2 teaspoon salt
1/2 teaspoon freshly ground pepper
6 slices bacon, crisp-cooked, crumbled

Heat the olive oil in a large saucepan over a medium flame. Add the onion and garlic and cook until light brown. Add the green chiles, black-eyed peas, diced tomatoes and beef broth and mix well. Add the salt and pepper and mix thoroughly. Cook until heated through. Ladle into soup bowls and sprinkle with bacon.

Yield: 10 to 12 servings

Energy Saver: Cooking outside on the gas grill saves energy required for cooling inside.

Broccoli and Crab Bisque

1/4 cup (1/2 stick) margarine
1 cup sliced leeks
1 cup sliced fresh mushrooms
1 cup fresh or frozen chopped broccoli
1 garlic clove, minced
1/4 cup flour
1/4 teaspoon thyme
1/8 teaspoon pepper
1 small bay leaf
3 cups chicken broth
1 cup light cream
1 (6-ounce) package frozen crab meat, thawed, drained
3/4 cup (3 ounces) shredded Jarlsberg or Swiss cheese

Melt the margarine in a large saucepan over a low flame. Add the leeks, mushrooms, broccoli and garlic and cook until tender-crisp, stirring constantly.

Add the flour, thyme, pepper and bay leaf and mix well. Add the chicken broth and cream all at once and mix well. Cook until the soup thickens and bubbles, stirring constantly.

Add the crab meat and cook until heated through. Ladle into soup bowls and sprinkle with cheese.

Yield: 6 to 8 servings

Golden Cauliflower Soup

6 cups water
1 teaspoon salt
1 large head cauliflower, broken into florets
1/2 cup (1 stick) margarine
1 cup finely chopped green onions
2 tablespoons flour
2 cups whole milk, or 1 cup milk and 1 cup half-and-half, warmed
2 cups (8 ounces) shredded sharp Cheddar cheese
1 teaspoon salt
1/8 teaspoon white pepper
1/8 teaspoon Tabasco sauce
1 tablespoon Worcestershire sauce
2 tablespoons lemon juice

Combine the water, 1 teaspoon salt and cauliflower in a large saucepan. Cook, uncovered, over a medium flame for 25 minutes or until the cauliflower is tender.

Melt the margarine in a large skillet. Add the green onions and cook for 7 minutes, stirring frequently. Reduce the flame to low, add the flour and cook for 2 minutes, stirring frequently. Add the milk gradually, stirring constantly. Add the cheese and cook until the cheese melts, stirring frequently.

Purée the cauliflower with the cooking liquid in a blender or food processor and return the mixture to the saucepan. Add the cheese sauce and stir to mix well. Add 1 teaspoon salt, pepper, Tabasco sauce, Worcestershire sauce and lemon juice and mix well. Heat to serving temperature and ladle into soup bowls. Garnish with grated cheese, chopped green onions and paprika. May chill the soup for several hours and serve cold.

Yield: 8 servings

Chicken Soup Parmigiana

8 ounces boneless skinless chicken breasts
1 envelope chicken noodle soup mix
2^1/$_2$ cups water
^{1}/$_2$ teaspoon oregano
^{1}/$_2$ teaspoon basil
^{1}/$_2$ teaspoon garlic powder
1 cup chopped fresh tomatoes, or 1 (8-ounce) can whole
    peeled tomatoes, chopped
1 cup sliced zucchini or yellow squash
^{1}/$_3$ cup shredded Parmesan or mozzarella cheese

Cut the chicken into ^{1}/$_2$-inch pieces. Combine the soup mix, water, oregano, basil and garlic powder in a large saucepan and mix well. Add the chicken, tomatoes and zucchini and mix well. Bring to a boil over a medium flame. Reduce the flame and cook for 20 minutes or until the chicken is cooked through, stirring occasionally. Ladle into soup bowls and sprinkle with cheese.

Yield: 4 or 5 servings

As quickly as a frog can
    jump,
Home Service will be at
    your door,
Call us when you're up
    a stump
'Cause that's the very
    thing we're for.

No matter how the Home Service Department got its gas message out, it always used a common hook: Bring people together with great recipes and good food.

The "Home Service Frog" was the mascot used in the mid-1930s on the Recipe of the Month card. Thousands of recipes were tested. And just like the department itself, the recipes evolved over the years to reflect customer needs and lifestyles.

Quick Chicken Gumbo

2 tablespoons margarine
1 small onion, chopped
1 green bell pepper, chopped
2 (14-ounce) cans chicken broth
1 cup mild picante sauce

1 cup frozen corn
2 cups nonfat sour cream
4 boneless skinless chicken breasts, cooked, shredded
4 cups hot cooked rice

Melt the margarine in a large saucepan over a low flame. Add the onion and green pepper and cook until tender. Add the broth, picante sauce and corn and cook for 5 minutes.

Place the sour cream in a bowl and stir in 1 cup of the hot broth gradually. Stir the sour cream mixture into the soup. Add the chicken and simmer for 5 to 8 minutes or until heated through. Divide the rice among 6 soup bowls. Ladle the hot soup over the rice.

Yield: 6 servings

Chicken Tortilla Soup

1 envelope chicken noodle soup mix
$2^1/_2$ cups water
1 (14-ounce) can whole peeled tomatoes, chopped
1 (4-ounce) can chopped green chiles

1 medium onion, chopped
1 cup chopped cooked chicken or turkey
$1/_2$ teaspoon cumin (optional)
1 cup crumbled tortilla chips

Combine the soup mix, water, tomatoes, green chiles, onion, chicken and cumin in a medium saucepan and mix well. Bring to a boil over a medium flame. Reduce the flame and cook for 8 minutes, stirring occasionally. Ladle into soup bowls. Top with the crushed tortilla chips. Garnish with a sprinkle of shredded Monterey Jack cheese.

Yield: 8 servings

Southern-Style Corn Chowder

2 ounces lean salt pork, diced
1/2 cup (1 stick) unsalted margarine
3 large onions, chopped
1 large green bell pepper, chopped
8 medium potatoes, peeled, diced
4 cups milk
2 cups heavy cream
5 cups fresh corn
1/4 cup minced fresh parsley
Salt and freshly ground pepper to taste
Freshly grated nutmeg to taste

Cook the salt pork in a large skillet over a low flame until 2 tablespoons fat have been rendered. Remove any remaining solid pork and add 2 tablespoons of the margarine. Heat until margarine melts. Add the onions and cook until light golden, stirring frequently. Add the green pepper and cook until tender and bright green. Remove the skillet from the flame and set aside.

Combine the potatoes with enough water to cover in a saucepan. Bring to a boil and cook just until the potatoes are tender. Drain well.

Combine the milk and cream in a large saucepan and heat over a low flame until heated through, stirring occasionally. Add the cooked onion and green pepper, potatoes, corn, parsley, salt, pepper and nutmeg and stir to mix well. Simmer for 10 minutes and remove from the flame.

Let stand for 3 hours or longer to cool and thicken. (Soup may be refrigerated, covered, overnight if desired.) Reheat the soup over a low flame. Stir in the remaining 6 tablespoons margarine gently to avoid mashing the vegetables. May stir in a small amount of milk for thinner soup if desired. Ladle into soup bowls and pass crumbled crisp-cooked bacon for garnish.

Yield: 12 servings

Crab Chowder

2 tablespoons margarine
1 cup sliced celery
1 medium onion, coarsely chopped
2 tablespoons flour
1/4 teaspoon thyme
1/4 teaspoon white pepper

5 cups skim milk
3 large potatoes, peeled, diced
1 (8-ounce) package crab meat, drained, flaked
6 slices crisp-cooked bacon, crumbled

Melt the margarine in a large saucepan over a medium flame. Add the celery and onion and cook until tender, stirring occasionally. Add the flour, thyme and pepper and mix well. Add the milk gradually, stirring constantly.

Add the potatoes and simmer until tender. Stir in the crab meat and cook until heated through. Ladle into soup bowls and sprinkle with the crumbled bacon.

Yield: 4 servings

Wild Rice Mushroom Soup

1 (10-ounce) package wild rice
1 tablespoon margarine
8 ounces fresh mushrooms, sliced
1/4 cup finely chopped onion
1/4 cup finely grated carrots
1/4 cup flour

1 (14-ounce) can chicken broth
1 tablespoon tomato paste
1 (12-ounce) can evaporated skim milk, or 1 1/2 cups skim milk
2 tablespoons sherry (optional)

Prepare the wild rice according to the package directions and set aside. Melt the margarine in a saucepan over a low flame. Add the mushrooms, onion and carrots and cook until tender, stirring constantly. Combine the flour and 1/2 cup of the chicken broth in a small bowl and blend until smooth. Add the remaining broth and stir to mix well. Pour the broth mixture into the vegetable mixture and cook until thickened, stirring constantly.

Add the tomato paste and mix well. Add the milk and rice and cook until heated through. Add the sherry and stir to mix well. Ladle into soup bowls and garnish with minced fresh parsley.

Yield: 4 to 6 servings

French Onion Soup

3 pounds yellow onions, thinly sliced
1/3 cup margarine, melted
1/4 cup vegetable oil
1/4 cup flour
12 cups beef broth
1 teaspoon salt
Freshly ground pepper to taste
1 teaspoon sugar
1/4 cup dry vermouth or cognac (optional)
Butter
6 slices French bread
1 cup (4 ounces) grated Gruyère or Parmesan cheese
Freshly grated nutmeg to taste (optional)

Combine the onions, margarine and oil in a Dutch oven and cook over a low flame for 20 to 25 minutes or just until golden. Sprinkle the flour over the onions and cook until golden brown, stirring constantly. Add the beef broth, salt, pepper, sugar and vermouth and mix well. Simmer for 45 minutes.

Butter the bread on both sides and toast. Preheat the gas broiler. Ladle the soup into ovenproof bowls and top with toasted bread. Sprinkle the bread slices with cheese and nutmeg. Broil 4 to 5 inches from the flame for 1 to 2 minutes or until the cheese is light brown.

Yield: 6 servings

Energy Saver: *Bake casseroles and desserts in large batches, doubling recipes; freeze extras for later use.*

Cinnamon Apple Salad

1 1/2 cups boiling water
1 1/2 cups sugar
3/4 cup red hot cinnamon candies

8 medium apples, pared, cored
3 ounces cream cheese, softened
1/3 cup chopped nuts

Combine the water, sugar and candies in a large saucepan and cook over a low flame until the candies dissolve, stirring frequently. Add the apples, cover and simmer until tender, turning carefully occasionally. Remove the apples carefully, drain and place on a plate. Cover and chill. Combine the cream cheese and nuts in a bowl and mix well. Fill the apple centers with the cream cheese mixture just before serving.

Yield: 8 servings

Apple Peanut Salad

1 (20-ounce) can pineapple chunks
2 cups miniature marshmallows
1 tablespoon flour
1/2 cup sugar
1 1/2 tablespoons white vinegar

1 egg, beaten
12 ounces whipped topping
2 large apples, chopped
1 1/2 cups Spanish peanuts

Drain the pineapple, reserving the juice. Combine the pineapple and marshmallows in a medium bowl and mix well. Chill, covered, overnight. Combine the pineapple juice, flour, sugar, vinegar and egg in a medium saucepan and cook over a low flame until the mixture thickens, stirring constantly. Chill, covered, overnight.

Combine the cooked sauce and whipped topping and mix well. Fold in the pineapple mixture, apples and peanuts. Chill, covered, for 3 hours or longer.

Yield: 6 servings

Cherry-Cola Salad

1 (17-ounce) can pitted dark sweet cherries
1 (20-ounce) can crushed pineapple
1 (3-ounce) package black cherry gelatin
1 (3-ounce) package raspberry gelatin
1 (12-ounce) can cola, chilled

1 cup finely chopped celery
1 cup pecans, chopped
1/2 cup flaked coconut (optional)
6 ounces cream cheese, softened

Drain the cherries and pineapple, reserving the juices. Add enough water to the reserved juice to measure 2 cups. Pour the liquid into a saucepan and bring it to a boil over a medium flame. Add the gelatin and mix until gelatin dissolves. Add the cola and stir to mix well. Pour into a large bowl. Chill, covered, until slightly thickened.

Combine the celery, pecans, cherries, pineapple and coconut in a medium bowl. Beat the cream cheese in a small bowl until fluffy and add to the fruit mixture, stirring to coat well. Fold the cream cheese and fruit mixture into the gelatin. Pour into a 9×13-inch pan and chill until firm. Cut into squares before serving.

Yield: 15 servings

Cranberry Salad

1 pound cranberries
2 cups sugar
1 cup tokay grapes, peeled, seeded

1 (8-ounce) can crushed pineapple, drained
1 cup pecans, chopped
1/2 pint whipping cream, whipped

Grind the cranberries in a food processor. Add the sugar, stir to mix well and let stand overnight. Add the grapes, pineapple and pecans and mix well. Fold the whipped cream into the fruit mixture just before serving. Serve as a dessert or as a side dish with turkey and dressing.

Yield: 8 servings

Frozen Fruit Salad

1 tablespoon unflavored gelatin
2 tablespoons lemon juice
3 ounces cream cheese, softened
1/4 cup mayonnaise

1/2 cup chopped nuts
1 (30-ounce) can fruit cocktail, drained
2/3 cup whipping cream
1/2 cup sugar

Soften the gelatin in the lemon juice in a heatproof cup for 5 minutes. Place the gelatin over hot water and heat until dissolved, stirring constantly. Combine the cream cheese and mayonnaise in a large bowl and blend well. Add the gelatin and blend well. Add the nuts and fruit cocktail and mix well.

Whip the cream in a medium bowl, adding the sugar gradually. Fold the whipped cream into the cream cheese mixture. Pour into an 8-inch pan, cover with plastic wrap and freeze until firm.

Yield: 8 to 10 servings

Millionaire Salad

3 ounces cream cheese, softened
2 tablespoons light cream
1/3 cup mayonnaise
2 tablespoons lemon juice
1/8 teaspoon salt
2 tablespoons sugar
1 cup diced pineapple

1 cup orange sections
1/2 cup maraschino cherry halves
1/2 cup light sweet cherry quarters
1/2 cup pecans
1 cup miniature marshmallows
1 cup whipping cream, whipped

Combine the cream cheese, light cream and mayonnaise in a bowl and blend well. Add the lemon juice, salt and sugar and mix well. Add the pineapple, orange sections, cherries, pecans and marshmallows and stir to coat well. Fold the whipped cream into the fruit mixture. Pour into an 8-inch pan, cover with plastic wrap and freeze until firm.

Yield: 8 to 10 servings

In-the-Pink Salad

1 (20-ounce) can crushed pineapple
1 cup water
1 (6-ounce) package strawberry gelatin
1 (16-ounce) can whole cranberry sauce
1/4 teaspoon nutmeg

1/4 teaspoon salt
1 teaspoon grated lemon zest
3 tablespoons lemon juice
2 cups sour cream
1/2 cup chopped pecans

Drain the pineapple, reserving the juice. Set the pineapple aside. Combine the pineapple juice, water and gelatin in a medium saucepan. Bring to a boil over a medium flame, stirring until the gelatin dissolves. Pour into a bowl and stir in the cranberry sauce, nutmeg, salt, lemon zest and lemon juice. Chill until slightly thickened.

Add the sour cream and mix well. Fold in the pineapple and pecans. Pour into a 2-quart mold and chill until firm. Invert the gelatin onto a lettuce-lined plate.

Yield: 8 to 10 servings

Strawberry Pretzel Surprise

2 cups crushed pretzels
3/4 cup (1 1/2 sticks) margarine, melted
3 tablespoons sugar
1 (6-ounce) package strawberry gelatin
2 cups boiling water

2 (10-ounce) packages frozen strawberries
8 ounces cream cheese, softened
1 cup plus 1 tablespoon sugar
8 ounces whipped topping

Preheat the gas oven to 400 degrees. Combine the pretzels, margarine and 3 tablespoons sugar and mix well. Press the mixture into the bottom of a lightly greased 9×13-inch baking dish. Bake for 6 minutes.

Combine the gelatin and boiling water in a large bowl and stir to dissolve. Stir in the strawberries and chill until slightly thickened. Beat the cream cheese and 1 cup plus 1 tablespoon sugar in a medium bowl until fluffy. Add the strawberry mixture and mix well. Fold in the whipped topping and spread evenly over the cooled pretzel crust. Chill, covered, until firm.

Yield: 10 servings

Ambrosia Chicken Salad

2 cups chopped cooked chicken
1 cup chopped celery
1 (11-ounce) can mandarin oranges, drained
1/2 cup green grape halves
1/2 cup chopped cashews or sliced almonds
Sour Cream Italian Salad Dressing (below)

Combine the chicken, celery, oranges, grapes and cashews in a large bowl and toss to mix well. Pour the Sour Cream Italian Salad Dressing over the chicken mixture and toss gently to coat. Chill, covered, for 2 to 3 hours.

Yield: 4 servings

Sour Cream Italian Salad Dressing

1/4 cup mayonnaise or nonfat mayonnaise
1/4 cup sour cream or nonfat sour cream
1 1/2 teaspoons Italian salad dressing mix

Combine the mayonnaise, sour cream and salad dressing mix in a small bowl and mix well.

Energy Saver: Replace the furnace filter every two or three months. Check the fan belts; replace when necessary.

Ramen Noodle Salad

1 (3-ounce) package ramen noodles, crumbled
1 (3-ounce) package slivered almonds
1/2 head napa cabbage, coarsely chopped
4 green onions, chopped

1 (11-ounce) can mandarin oranges, drained
4 boneless skinless chicken breasts, cooked, diced
Oriental Salad Dressing (below)

Preheat the gas oven to 350 degrees. Reserve the oriental spice mix from the ramen noodles for the Oriental Salad Dressing. Spread the noodles and almonds evenly in the bottom of a lightly greased 9×13-inch baking dish. Bake for 10 minutes. Cool completely.

Combine the napa cabbage, green onions, oranges, chicken and baked noodle mixture in a large bowl and mix well. Pour the Oriental Salad Dressing over the salad and toss gently.

Yield: 8 servings

Oriental Salad Dressing

1/4 cup canola oil
3 tablespoons vinegar
2 tablespoons sugar

Oriental spice mix
1/2 teaspoon salt
Pepper to taste

Combine the canola oil, vinegar, sugar, spice mix, salt and pepper in a small bowl and mix well until the sugar dissolves. Chill, covered, in the refrigerator until ready for use.

Energy Saver: Use the correct heat setting or cycle for fabrics to be dried in the dryer.

Marinated Shrimp Salad

2 quarts water
2¹/₂ pounds unpeeled medium fresh shrimp
1 green bell pepper, coarsely chopped
4 green onions with tops, sliced
¹/₂ cup sliced celery
¹/₂ cup unpeeled cucumber, chopped
1 (2-ounce) jar diced pimento, drained
Spicy Apple Marinade (below)
¹/₃ pound snow peas

Bring the water to a boil in a large saucepan over a medium flame. Add the shrimp. Cook for 3 to 5 minutes or until the shrimp turn pink. Drain, rinse with cold water, peel, devein and chill.

Combine the chilled shrimp, green pepper, green onions, celery, cucumber and pimento in a large shallow dish and mix well. Pour the Spicy Apple Marinade over the shrimp mixture and toss to mix well. Chill, covered, overnight.

Place the snow peas on a steaming rack over boiling water. Steam, covered, for 3 to 5 minutes or until tender-crisp. Rinse with cold water, drain well and chill. Serve the shrimp salad over a bed of snow peas.

Yield: 6 servings

Spicy Apple Marinade

1 cup unsweetened apple juice
1 teaspoon salt
²/₃ cup cider vinegar
¹/₄ teaspoon hot red pepper sauce
¹/₄ teaspoon paprika

Combine the apple juice, salt, vinegar, hot red pepper sauce and paprika in a small bowl and mix well.

Tuna Salad Sandwiches

1/4 cup chopped pecans
1 (6-ounce) can albacore tuna, drained
3 ounces cream cheese, softened

1/4 cup chopped celery
1 teaspoon lemon pepper
3 croissants

Preheat the gas oven to 300 degrees. Spread the pecans on a baking sheet and toast for 5 minutes. Combine the tuna, cream cheese, pecans, celery and lemon pepper in a bowl and mix well.

Slice the croissants lengthwise and spread with the tuna mixture. Serve garnished with baby greens.

Yield: 3 servings

Artichoke and Rice Salad

1 (6-ounce) package long grain and wild rice
    mix
1 (14-ounce) can artichoke hearts, drained,
    chopped
1 (2-ounce) jar diced pimento, drained

12 pimento-stuffed olives, chopped
3 green onions with tops, chopped
1 cup chopped celery
1/2 cup mayonnaise
1 teaspoon curry powder

Cook the rice mix according to the package directions, omitting the butter. Cool completely. Combine the artichoke hearts, pimento, olives, green onions, celery and rice in a bowl and toss to mix well.

Blend the mayonnaise with the curry powder. Add to the rice mixture and toss to mix well. Chill, covered, until serving time. Serve garnished with tomato wedges.

Yield: 8 servings

Guacamole

2 ripe avocados
3 tablespoons lemon juice
2 tablespoons mayonnaise
2 to 3 tablespoons minced onion

1 tomato, peeled, finely chopped
3 or 4 drops Tabasco sauce
3/4 teaspoon salt
Freshly ground pepper to taste

Peel the avocados and mash in a bowl until smooth. Reserve the seeds. Add the lemon juice and mayonnaise and blend well. Add the onion, tomato, Tabasco sauce, salt and pepper and mix well.

Place the avocado seeds in the guacamole to prevent discoloration and press plastic wrap over the surface to seal out air. Chill, covered, for several hours.

Remove the seeds and place the guacamole in a serving bowl. Garnish with a dollop of sour cream, minced green onions and sliced ripe olives.

Yield: 4 servings

Three-Bean Salad

1 (16-ounce) can French-style green beans
1 (16-ounce) can yellow wax beans
1 (16-ounce) can red kidney beans
1/2 cup finely chopped green bell pepper
1/2 cup minced onion

1/2 cup vegetable oil
1/2 cup cider vinegar
3/4 cup sugar
1 teaspoon salt
1/2 teaspoon pepper

Drain the beans well. Combine the beans, green pepper and onion and mix well. Combine the oil, vinegar, sugar, salt and pepper in a bottle or bowl and mix until the sugar and salt are completely dissolved. Add the vinegar mixture to the bean mixture and toss well to mix. Chill, covered, for 1 to 4 hours.

Yield: 12 servings

Layered Salad

4 cups torn salad greens
1 cup thinly sliced red onion
$1/2$ cup chopped celery
$1/2$ cup coarsely chopped green bell pepper
$1 1/2$ cups cauliflower florets
1 (10-ounce) package frozen peas, thawed, drained
8 ounces crisp-cooked bacon, crumbled
2 teaspoons fines herbes or salad seasoning
Freshly ground pepper to taste
1 cup mayonnaise
$2/3$ cup grated Parmesan cheese

Place a layer of half the salad greens in a large glass salad bowl. Arrange the onion rings around the outer edge of the bowl. Mix the celery and green pepper together. Layer half the celery mixture over the salad greens. Add layers of the cauliflower, peas and the remaining celery mixture. Sprinkle with the bacon and cover with a layer of the remaining greens. Sprinkle with the herbs and pepper.

Spread the mayonnaise over the top, sealing to the edge of the bowl. Sprinkle with the cheese and chill, covered, for 8 hours or overnight.

Yield: 8 servings

In the late 1930s, the logo on the Recipe of the Month evolved into "Little Bill." Little Bill introduced recipes each month until 1942. He also had energy-saving tips and a limerick with each recipe.

Someone asked
"What's in a name?"
Said Little Bill
"The answer is plain
I modestly say,
Mine's brought me fame
For the service I render
With the little blue flame!"

Nine-Day Slaw

1 (3-pound) head cabbage
1 green bell pepper
2 medium onions
2 cups sugar
1 cup vegetable oil

1 cup vinegar
2 tablespoons celery seeds
2 tablespoons salt
2 tablespoons sugar

Shred the cabbage, green pepper and onions. Place in a large bowl. Add 2 cups sugar and toss to mix well.

Combine the oil, vinegar, celery seeds, salt and 2 tablespoons sugar in a saucepan and bring to a boil over a medium flame, stirring constantly. Pour the hot liquid over the cabbage mixture immediately and mix well. Let stand until cooled completely. Chill, covered, for up to 9 days.

Yield: 10 to 12 servings

Gwin's Kraut Salad

1 1/2 cups sugar
1/2 cup vinegar
1 (32-ounce) can sauerkraut
1/2 cup chopped green bell pepper

1/4 cup chopped red bell pepper
1/2 cup chopped onion
1/2 cup chopped celery

Combine the sugar and vinegar in a saucepan and bring to a boil over a medium flame, stirring occasionally until the sugar dissolves. Let stand until cooled completely.

Drain the sauerkraut well. Combine the sauerkraut, green and red peppers, onion and celery in a large bowl and toss lightly to mix. Pour the cooled vinegar mixture over the vegetables and mix well. Chill, covered, for 24 hours. May store in the refrigerator for several weeks.

Yield: 6 servings

Okra and Tomato Salad

1 (16-ounce) package frozen okra
3 tablespoons canola oil
2 cups cherry tomato halves
1 cup sliced celery
2 tablespoons chopped green onions
Zesty Salad Dressing (below)

Cook the okra in the canola oil in a large skillet over a medium flame until light brown. Drain well and cool completely. Combine the cooked okra, tomatoes, celery and green onions in a large bowl and toss gently to mix. Pour the desired amount of Zesty Salad Dressing over the vegetable mixture and toss to mix. Serve the salad on a bed of assorted lettuce with the remaining Zesty Salad Dressing on the side.

Yield: 8 servings

Zesty Salad Dressing

1/4 cup cider vinegar
2 tablespoons dry white wine
2 teapoons soy sauce
1 teaspoon sugar
1 teaspoon dry mustard
1/2 teaspoon salt
1/8 teaspoon red pepper flakes
1/4 teaspoon minced garlic
2/3 cup canola oil

Combine the vinegar, white wine, soy sauce, sugar, dry mustard, salt, red pepper flakes and garlic in a blender. Add the canola oil in a fine stream, processing constantly at a high speed until smooth.

Tabouli

1 cup cracked wheat
2 pounds fresh tomatoes, chopped
1 medium bunch parsley, chopped
1 bunch green onions, chopped

1/2 cup chopped cucumber (optional)
1/2 cup fresh lemon juice
1/2 cup vegetable oil
Salt to taste

Rinse the cracked wheat with hot water and drain well; do not soak. Combine the cracked wheat, tomatoes, parsley, green onions and cucumber in a bowl and mix well.

Add the lemon juice, oil and salt and mix well. Pack the mixture into a large container. Chill, covered, for several hours.

Yield: 4 to 6 servings

Celery Seed Dressing

1/2 cup sugar
1 teaspoon salt
1 teaspoon dry mustard
1/2 teaspoon paprika

1/2 teaspoon celery seeds
2 tablespoons grated onion
1/4 cup vinegar
1 cup vegetable oil

Combine the sugar, salt, dry mustard, paprika and celery seeds in a bowl and mix well. Add the grated onion and vinegar and mix well. Add the oil gradually, beating constantly. Chill, covered, until ready to use.

Yield: 1 1/2 cups

Energy Saver: *Open the oven door only long enough to put in or take out foods. Use the timer to time foods; make notes on the time required when baking two or more foods requiring different times.*

Parsley Vinaigrette

1 cup vegetable oil
1 cup chopped fresh parsley
1/2 cup fresh lemon juice
1/4 cup chopped chives

1 teaspoon sugar
1 teaspoon salt
1 garlic clove

Combine the oil, parsley, lemon juice, chives, sugar, salt and garlic in a blender and process for 1 minute or until smooth. Pour into a bottle or jar. Chill, covered, until ready to use.

Yield: 2 cups

Poppy Seed Dressing

3/4 cup sugar
1 teaspoon dry mustard
1 teaspoon salt
1/3 cup vinegar

1 1/2 tablespoons onion juice
1 cup vegetable oil
1 1/2 tablespoons poppy seeds

Combine the sugar, dry mustard, salt and vinegar in a bowl and mix well. Add the onion juice and beat vigorously to mix. Add the oil gradually, beating constantly until thickened. Add the poppy seeds and mix well. Chill, covered, until ready to use. This dressing is especially delicious on fruit salads.

Yield: 1 3/4 cups

Sooner Salad Dressing

1 quart mayonnaise
2/3 cup evaporated milk
1 tablespoon Worcestershire sauce
1 tablespoon white vinegar

2 tablespoons sugar
2 tablespoons garlic powder
1 cup (4 ounces) shredded sharp Cheddar
   cheese

Combine the mayonnaise, evaporated milk, Worcestershire sauce, white vinegar, sugar and garlic powder and blend well. Add the cheese and mix well. Chill, covered, until ready to use.

Yield: 1 quart

While statehood was being considered and the legislation formulated, the discovery of oil and natural gas began to provide an economic magnet that attracted numerous business interests to the territory.

Entrees

Smoky Beef Brisket

1 (5- to 6-pound) beef brisket
1 teaspoon meat tenderizer
1/4 cup liquid smoke
1 teaspoon pepper
1 teaspoon celery salt
1 teaspoon garlic salt

1 teaspoon onion powder
1 teaspoon paprika
1 teaspoon nutmeg
1/4 cup packed brown sugar
1/2 cup barbecue sauce

Sprinkle the brisket with meat tenderizer, liquid smoke and pepper. Wrap in heavy-duty foil and chill overnight. Preheat the gas oven to 300 degrees. Combine the celery salt, garlic salt, onion powder, paprika, nutmeg and brown sugar in a small bowl and mix well. Spread the mixture over the brisket and rewrap tightly. Bake for 1 hour.

Reduce the temperature to 250 degrees and bake for 4 to 5 hours, or until cooked through. Drain and reserve the cooking juices. Slice the brisket across the grain into thin slices and place in a baking dish. Combine 1 cup of the reserved brisket liquid with the barbecue sauce in a medium bowl and pour over the slices. Reheat in a 275-degree gas oven for 45 minutes.

Yield: 12 servings

Touchdown Tenderloin

2 tablespoons Dijon mustard
1 tablespoon olive oil
1 (4-pound) beef tenderloin, trimmed
1 tablespoon freshly ground pepper
1 tablespoon dried oregano, crushed

1 tablespoon dried thyme, crushed
1 tablespoon finely chopped fresh chives
2 garlic cloves, minced
1 teaspoon salt

Combine the Dijon mustard and olive oil in a small bowl, mix well and brush onto the tenderloin on all sides. Combine the pepper, oregano, thyme, chives, garlic and salt and mix well. Pat the tenderloin with the seasonings. Place on a rack in a large shallow roasting pan and let stand at room temperature for 30 minutes. Preheat the gas oven to 425 degrees. Roast for 45 minutes or until a meat thermometer registers 140 degrees for rare or to the desired doneness. Let stand for 15 minutes before slicing.

Yield: 12 servings

Baked Corned Beef with Peppered Cabbage

1 (3- to 4-pound) corned beef brisket
3/4 cup sugar
1/2 teaspoon ground ginger
1/2 teaspoon ground cloves
1/2 teaspoon dry mustard
1 tablespoon honey
Peppered Cabbage (below)

Combine the brisket with enough water to cover in a large pot and boil, covered, for 2 to 3 hours or until tender. Drain, trim excess fat and place the brisket in a large heavy baking pan.

Preheat the gas oven to 325 degrees. Combine the sugar, ginger, cloves, dry mustard and honey in a small bowl, mix well and spread over the brisket. Bake for 25 to 30 minutes. Slice across the grain into thin slices. Serve with the Peppered Cabbage.

Yield: 6 servings

Peppered Cabbage

1/4 cup (1/2 stick) margarine
1 medium head white cabbage, grated
2 tablespoons sour cream
1 teaspoon freshly ground pepper
Salt to taste

Melt the margarine in a large skillet over a medium flame. Add the cabbage and cook for 2 to 3 minutes or until tender-crisp, stirring constantly. Add the sour cream, pepper and salt and stir well to mix.

Energy Saver: Use the flame height best suited to the pan, turning so the flame does not extend beyond the edge of the pan.

Marinated Flank Steak

2 (1½-pound) flank steaks
¼ cup soy sauce
3 tablespoons honey
2 tablespoons red wine vinegar

1½ teaspoons garlic powder
1½ teaspoons ground ginger
¾ cup vegetable oil
1 green onion, finely chopped

Trim the steaks and score diagonally in a diamond pattern. Combine the soy sauce, honey, vinegar, garlic powder and ginger in a bottle, seal and shake vigorously. Add the oil and green onion and shake to mix well. Place the steaks in a shallow dish, add the marinade and marinate, covered, in the refrigerator for 4 hours or longer.

Preheat the gas grill or gas broiler using a medium flame. Drain the steaks and place on the grill or rack in a broiler pan. Grill for 6 minutes per side for medium-rare. Slice thinly on the diagonal. May substitute sirloin, chuck or round steak for the flank steak if desired.

Yield: 4 servings

Lemon Pepper Steak Pinwheels

½ cup vegetable oil
⅔ cup water
¼ cup soy sauce
2 teaspoons Worcestershire sauce

2 or 3 drops Tabasco sauce
1 tablespoon lemon pepper
2 (2- to 2½-pound) flank steaks
8 cherry tomatoes or mushroom caps

Combine the oil, water, soy sauce, Worcestershire sauce, Tabasco sauce and lemon pepper in a small bowl and whisk to mix well. Pound the steaks into ¼-inch thickness, cut into eight 2-inch wide strips and place in a shallow dish. Pour the marinade over the steak strips and marinate in the refrigerator for several hours, turning occasionally.

Preheat the gas grill using a medium flame. Drain the steak strips and roll each strip loosely around a cherry tomato or mushroom cap as for a jelly roll, securing with wooden picks. Place the steak pinwheels on the grill, close the grill cover and grill for 20 to 25 minutes, turning once.

Yield: 8 to 10 servings

Steak Diane

1/4 cup (1/2 stick) butter
1/4 cup chopped green onions with tops
2 tablespoons finely chopped parsley
2 tablespoons steak sauce
1/4 cup sherry or madeira
2 tablespoons Worcestershire sauce

4 (1/4- to 1/3-inch thick) sirloin or boneless
  club steaks
Salt and pepper to taste
2 tablespoons butter
1/2 cup cognac, warmed

Combine 1/4 cup butter, green onions, parsley, steak sauce, sherry and Worcestershire sauce in a small saucepan and heat over a low flame for 1 minute, mix well and set aside.

Season the steaks with salt and pepper. Melt 1 tablespoon butter in a large skillet over a medium flame. Add the steaks 2 at a time and cook for 3 minutes, turning once.

Arrange the 4 steaks in the skillet. Top with the sauce and cook until bubbly. Drizzle the cognac into the skillet, ignite and spoon over the steaks. Serve immediately.

Yield: 4 servings

Teriyaki Beef

2 pounds sirloin tip steak
1/2 cup soy sauce
1/2 cup finely chopped green onions
1/4 cup packed brown sugar

1 garlic clove, crushed
1/4 teaspoon pepper
1/4 teaspoon ground ginger

Trim the steak and pound into 1/4-inch thickness and score. Cut into 1 1/2-inch wide strips and place in a shallow baking dish. Combine the soy sauce, green onions, brown sugar, garlic, pepper and ginger in a small bowl and mix well. Pour over the steak and marinate in the refrigerator for 1 hour.

Preheat the gas grill using a low to medium flame. Drain the steak and thread ripple-fashion onto skewers. Place on the grill and grill for 3 minutes on each side.

Yield: 4 to 6 servings

Stir-Fried Beef and Vegetables

1 pound flank steak
2 tablespoons soy sauce
2 tablespoons dry vermouth
2 garlic cloves, crushed
1/8 to 1/4 teaspoon crushed red pepper flakes
1 cup beef broth
2 teaspoons cornstarch
3 teaspoons vegetable oil
1 medium onion, thinly sliced
1 bunch broccoli, cut into 2-inch pieces
1 green bell pepper, cut into 1 1/2-inch pieces
3/4 cup beef broth
1/2 pint cherry tomatoes, cut into halves

Trim the steak and cut lengthwise into 1 1/2-inch strips and then diagonally across the grain into 1/8-inch slivers. Combine the soy sauce, vermouth, garlic and red pepper flakes in a large bowl and mix well. Add the steak and toss to coat well. Combine 1 cup beef broth and the cornstarch in a medium bowl and mix well. Set aside. Heat 2 teaspoons of the oil in a large skillet over a medium-high flame until very hot. Add the steak slivers and cook for 3 to 5 minutes, stirring constantly. Remove the steak and set aside.

Heat the remaining 1 teaspoon oil in the skillet. Add the onion, broccoli and green pepper and stir-fry for 2 to 3 minutes. Lower the flame and add 3/4 cup beef broth. Cover and cook for 5 minutes or until the vegetables are tender-crisp. Add the tomatoes, beef strips and cornstarch mixture. Cook until the sauce thickens, stirring constantly but gently. Serve over hot cooked rice.

Yield: 4 servings

Energy Saver: *Plan to bake several foods in the oven at the same time.*

Steak Fajitas

1/2 cup olive oil
1/4 cup red wine vinegar
1/3 cup lime juice
1/3 cup finely chopped onion
1 teaspoon sugar
1 teaspoon dried oregano leaves
1/2 teaspoon salt
1/2 teaspoon pepper
1/4 teaspoon cumin
3 garlic cloves, minced
2 pounds skirt steak or flank steak
Juice of 1 lemon (optional)
6 flour tortillas

Combine the olive oil, vinegar, lime juice, onion, sugar, oregano, salt, pepper, cumin and garlic in a small bowl and whisk to mix well. Pound the steak into 1/4-inch thickness and place in a shallow dish. Add the marinade, turning to coat the steak thoroughly, and marinate, covered, in the refrigerator for 8 hours or longer.

Preheat the grill using a medium flame. Drain the steak and grill for 6 to 7 minutes on each side or to desired doneness.

Preheat the gas oven to 325 degrees. Slice the steak across the grain into thin slices and drizzle with lemon juice. Wrap the tortillas in foil and bake for 15 minutes. Wrap the tortillas around the steak strips and garnish with salsa, guacamole, chopped tomatoes and sour cream.

Yield: 4 to 6 servings

KITCHENEERING
with the HOME SERVICE DEPARTMENT of
OKLAHOMA NATURAL
Gas Company

"Thanks to the Friendly Blue Flame" served the company for a short time. Then "Kitcheneering" became the logo and heading for the recipe printed each month. This logo lasted more than 50 years on the recipe sheets published for customers.

Beef Stroganoff Superb

1/4 cup (1/2 stick) margarine
16 ounces fresh mushrooms, sliced
1 onion, minced
2 pounds sirloin steak, cut into thin strips
2 (10-ounce) cans beef bouillon

1/4 cup ketchup
2 small garlic cloves, crushed
2 teaspoons salt
1/3 cup flour
1 to 2 cups sour cream

Melt the margarine in a skillet over a medium flame. Add the mushrooms and onion and cook until tender, stirring frequently. Remove the vegetables, add the steak and brown lightly, stirring frequently. Reserve 3/4 cup of the bouillon. Combine the ketchup, the remaining bouillon, garlic and salt in a medium bowl and mix well. Add to the skillet, cover and cook for 15 minutes, stirring occasionally.

Combine the reserved bouillon and flour in a small bowl and mix well. Add the bouillon and flour mixture to the skillet and mix well. Add the cooked mushrooms and onions and bring the mixture to a boil. Cook for 1 minute and reduce the flame. Add the desired amount of sour cream and mix well. Do not allow the mixture to boil after adding the sour cream. Serve over hot cooked rice or noodles.

Yield: 6 to 8 servings

Company Casserole

8 ounces medium noodles
1 1/2 pounds ground beef
1 teaspoon salt
Pepper to taste
1/4 teaspoon garlic salt
1 (8-ounce) can tomato sauce

1 cup cream-style cottage cheese
1 cup sour cream
6 green onions, chopped
3/4 cup (3 ounces) shredded sharp
    Cheddar cheese

Cook the noodles according to the package directions. Drain, rinse, drain well and set aside. Preheat the gas oven to 350 degrees. Brown the ground beef in a skillet over a medium flame, stirring until crumbly; drain. Add the salt, pepper, garlic salt and tomato sauce and mix well. Cook for 5 minutes or until bubbly. Combine the cottage cheese, sour cream, green onions and noodles in a bowl and toss to mix. Layer the noodles and ground beef mixture alternately in a lightly greased shallow 2-quart casserole. Top with cheese. Bake for 30 minutes.

Yield: 6 servings

Favorite Meat Loaf

1/4 cup shortening
2 small onions, minced
1/4 cup finely chopped green bell pepper
2 pounds ground round
2 cups soft bread crumbs
2 eggs, beaten
2 teaspoons salt
1 teaspoon dry mustard
2 tablespoons horseradish
3/4 cup ketchup
1/4 cup packed brown sugar

Preheat the gas oven to 350 degrees. Melt the shortening in a skillet over a medium flame. Add the onions and green pepper and cook for 10 minutes, stirring frequently. Combine the onions, green pepper, ground round, bread crumbs, eggs, salt, dry mustard, horseradish and 1/4 cup of the ketchup in a large bowl and mix well.

Press into a greased 5×10-inch loaf pan or shape into 4 small loaves and place in a shallow baking pan; do not allow loaves to touch. Bake the large loaf for 45 minutes or the small loaves for 30 minutes.

Combine the remaining 1/2 cup ketchup and brown sugar in a small bowl and mix well. Brush the loaf with the ketchup mixture and bake for 15 minutes longer.

Note: Meat loaf freezes well if cooled completely and wrapped in an airtight foil package. To reheat, place the unwrapped meat loaf in a baking dish, pour tomato juice around the loaf and bake until heated through.

Yield: 6 to 8 servings

Energy Saver: *Keep flames a clear blue with proper adjustment.*

Great Lasagna

1 1/2 pounds ground beef
3/4 cup chopped onion
3/4 cup chopped green bell pepper
3 (6-ounce) cans tomato paste
2 1/4 cups hot water
1 cup plus 2 tablespoons red burgundy wine
1 tablespoon salt
1 1/2 tablespoons minced parsley
1 tablespoon minced garlic
3/4 teaspoon basil
3 bay leaves
1 teaspoon oregano
3/4 teaspoon rosemary
1/2 teaspoon coarsely ground pepper
3 eggs, slightly beaten
4 cups cream-style cottage cheese, drained, or dry-curd cottage cheese
8 ounces lasagna noodles, cooked, drained
3 cups (12 ounces) shredded mozzarella cheese
1/3 to 1/2 cup grated Parmesan cheese

Brown the ground beef, onion and green pepper in a skillet over a medium flame until the ground beef is crumbly, stirring frequently; drain and set aside. Combine the tomato paste, water, wine, salt, parsley and garlic in a saucepan and mix well. Add the basil, bay leaves, oregano, rosemary and pepper and mix well. Bring to a boil over a medium flame. Add the ground beef mixture and simmer for 15 minutes, stirring occasionally. Remove and discard the bay leaves. Set the sauce aside.

Preheat the gas oven to 350 degrees. Combine the eggs and cottage cheese in a bowl and mix well. Layer the ground beef sauce, lasagna noodles, cottage cheese mixture and mozzarella cheese alternately in a lightly greased 9×13-inch baking dish, ending with the sauce. Top with Parmesan cheese. Bake for 40 to 45 minutes or until bubbly. Let stand for 10 to 15 minutes before cutting. May be prepared and baked ahead if desired; reheat, covered with foil, at 350 degrees for 25 to 30 minutes.

Yield: 10 to 12 servings

Mexican Pizza

1 1/2 cups buttermilk baking mix
1/2 cup yellow cornmeal
1/2 cup cold water
1 pound ground round
1 (4-ounce) can chopped green chiles
1 envelope taco seasoning mix
3/4 cup water
1 (16-ounce) can refried beans
1 1/2 cups (6 ounces) shredded low-fat Cheddar cheese
1 cup shredded lettuce
2 medium tomatoes, chopped
1/2 cup chopped onion

Preheat the gas oven to 425 degrees. Combine the baking
mix, cornmeal and 1/2 cup water in a bowl and mix well
until a dough forms. Pat the dough into a 12-inch circle on
a lightly greased pizza pan. Bake for 10 minutes.

Brown the ground round in a skillet over a medium
flame, stirring until crumbly; drain. Add the chiles, taco
seasoning mix and 3/4 cup water and bring to a boil, stirring
frequently. Cook for 5 to 10 minutes or until thickened,
stirring frequently.

Spread the beans over the crust, top with the ground beef
mixture and sprinkle with cheese. Bake for 10 minutes. Top
with lettuce, tomatoes and onion. Cut into wedges and
serve with taco sauce.

Yield: 12 servings

The ONG Home Service
Department got its start in
the gas industry during the
early 1930s. New appliances
were appearing in the
market and the industry
saw an opportunity to
increase gas usage while
improving customer
relations. Equipped with a
model kitchen, including
a gas range and Electrolux
gas refrigerator, a
demonstration room was
booked almost daily for
cooking classes. This area
was called the "Blue Flame
Room" and many were
located in major ONG
offices throughout the
state. Targeted audiences
included everyone from
housewives to Girl Scouts,
brides-to-be, and empty-
nesters.

Pork Chops with Knockwurst and Potatoes

1 tablespoon caraway seeds
1/2 teaspoon salt
1/4 teaspoon freshly ground pepper
6 (1/2-inch) center cut loin pork chops
1/2 cup flour
2 tablespoons shortening
8 ounces knockwurst
3 small sweet gherkins
1 cup coarsely chopped onion
1/2 cup coarsely chopped carrot
1/2 cup coarsely chopped celery
1 cup chicken stock or broth
4 large potatoes, peeled, thinly sliced
6 medium tomatoes, peeled, coarsely chopped

Combine the caraway seeds, salt and pepper and rub the pork chops with the mixture. Coat the chops with the flour, shaking off the excess. Melt the shortening in a large heavy skillet over a medium flame. Brown the chops for 10 minutes, turning once. Slice the knockwurst into 1/4-inch rounds.

Rinse the gherkins with cold water, drain well, chop finely and set aside. Remove the chops and combine the knockwurst, onion, carrot, celery and gherkins in the skillet. Cook for 5 minutes, stirring frequently.

Return the chops to the skillet and add enough stock to come to the top of the chops without covering. Arrange the potato slices evenly over the chops, covering completely. Top with the chopped tomatoes. Bring to a boil, cover, reduce the flame to low and cook for 45 minutes or until the potatoes are tender. Serve immediately.

Yield: 6 servings

Honey Mustard Pork Tenderloin

4 tablespoons honey
2 tablespoons cider vinegar
2 tablespoons brown sugar

1 tablespoon Dijon mustard
1 pork tenderloin

Preheat the gas grill using a medium flame. Combine the honey, vinegar, brown sugar and mustard in a small bowl and mix well. Reserve 1/4 cup of the sauce, and coat the tenderloin with the remaining mixture.

Grill for 15 to 20 minutes or until a meat thermometer registers 155 degrees, basting occasionally. Slice and serve with the reserved sauce.

Yield: 6 servings

Smothered Ham

1 (2-inch thick) center-cut ham slice
8 whole cloves
1 1/2 cups milk, scalded
1 1/2 cups dry bread crumbs

1/2 teaspoon salt
1/2 teaspoon cinnamon
1 1/2 tablespoons finely chopped onion
1/3 cup packed brown sugar

Combine the ham with enough water to cover in a large pot. Cook over a low flame for 45 minutes. Drain well and place in a lightly greased baking dish.

Preheat the gas oven to 350 degrees. Press the cloves into the ham. Combine the milk, bread crumbs, salt, cinnamon and onion in a medium bowl and mix well. Spread the mixture over the ham and sprinkle with the brown sugar. Bake for 50 minutes or until golden brown and crispy.

This recipe is a very old version dating from about 1857.

Yield: 4 to 6 servings

Ham Della Robbia

1 (8- to 10-pound) boneless ham
1 (16-ounce) can sliced peaches
1 (8-ounce) can crushed pineapple
2 tablespoons cornstarch
1/2 teaspoon cinnamon
Dash of ground cloves
1 cup water
1/3 cup frozen orange juice concentrate, thawed
1/2 cup maraschino cherries
1/4 cup light raisins
1/2 cup coarsely chopped pecans

Preheat the gas oven to 325 degrees. Place the ham in a baking dish and score into 1/4-inch deep diamonds. Bake for 1 1/2 to 2 hours.

Drain the peaches and pineapple, reserving the juices. Combine the fruit juices, cornstarch, cinnamon, cloves, water and orange juice concentrate in a saucepan and cook over a low flame until the mixture thickens and bubbles, stirring constantly. Spoon 1/4 of the mixture over the ham and bake for 30 minutes longer, basting occasionally.

Reserve several peach slices and cherries for garnish. Cut the remaining peaches into bite-size pieces and slice the remaining cherries. Add the peaches, pineapple, cherries, raisins and pecans to the sauce and cook over a low flame for 10 minutes, stirring frequently.

Remove the ham to a serving plate, garnish with the peach slices and whole cherries and spoon a small amount of the sauce over the top. Slice the ham and serve with the sauce.

Yield: 8 to 10 servings

Energy Saver: *Keep the damper closed when the fireplace is not in use. Use a glass fireplace screen.*

Glazed Individual Ham Loaves

1 pound sugar-cured ham, ground
1 pound very lean ground pork
2/3 cup cracker crumbs
2/3 cup milk

2 eggs, beaten
1 cup packed brown sugar
1 teaspoon dry mustard
3 tablespoons vinegar

Preheat the gas oven to 350 degrees. Combine the ham, pork, cracker crumbs and milk in a large bowl and mix well. Add the eggs and mix well. Shape the mixture into 4-inch loaves and place on a rack in a roasting pan. Bake for 30 minutes.

Combine the brown sugar, dry mustard and vinegar in a small saucepan and bring to a boil, stirring frequently. Pour the sauce over the loaves and bake for 15 minutes longer.

Yield: 6 servings

Sweet and Sauer Sausage Dinner

3 slices bacon
1 red onion, sliced
1 (16-ounce) can sauerkraut
1/2 teaspoon caraway seeds

1 1/2 pounds smoked Polish sausages
1 (20-ounce) can pineapple chunks
1 tablespoon lemon juice

Fry the bacon in a skillet until crisp. Reserve 1 tablespoon of the bacon drippings, drain, crumble and set aside. Combine the bacon drippings, onion, sauerkraut and caraway seeds in the skillet and cook over a medium flame for 2 minutes.

Bring a large pot of water to a boil and add the sausages. Cook for 5 minutes; drain. Drain the pineapple, reserving 1/4 cup of the liquid. Add the pineapple, reserved liquid, lemon juice and bacon to the sauerkraut, tossing to mix well. Top the sauerkraut mixture with the boiled sausages and cook, covered, for 10 minutes. Serve with boiled potatoes.

Yield: 4 servings

Crunchy Sausage Casserole

1 (6-ounce) package long grain and wild rice
   mix
1 pound bulk pork sausage
1 pound ground beef
1 cup chopped onion

1 (8-ounce) can sliced mushrooms
1 (8-ounce) can water chestnuts, drained,
   sliced
3 tablespoons soy sauce
1 (3-ounce) package sliced almonds

Prepare the rice mix according to the package instructions. Preheat the gas oven to 325 degrees. Combine the sausage, ground beef and onion in a large skillet and cook over a medium flame, stirring until brown and crumbly; drain.

Add the cooked rice, mushrooms, water chestnuts and soy sauce and stir to mix. Spoon the mixture into an ungreased 2-quart casserole. Sprinkle with the almonds. Bake, uncovered, for 50 minutes or until heated through. Garnish with lemon slices and parsley sprigs.

Yield: 8 to 10 servings

Breakfast Pizza

1 pound bulk pork sausage
1/2 cup chopped green bell pepper
1/2 cup chopped onion
1 (4-ounce) can sliced mushrooms, drained,
   or 1 cup sliced fresh mushrooms

1 (8-count) can crescent rolls
3/4 cup milk
4 eggs, beaten
2 cups (8 ounces) shredded mozzarella
   cheese

Preheat the gas oven to 325 degrees. Brown the sausage in a skillet, stirring until crumbly. Reserve a small amount of the drippings, drain the sausage well and set aside. Combine the reserved drippings, green pepper, onion and mushrooms in the skillet and cook until tender, stirring frequently. Return the sausage to the skillet and remove from the heat.

Unroll the crescent roll dough and press over the bottom and sides of a lightly greased 9×12-inch baking dish, pressing the perforations to seal. Combine the milk and eggs in a bowl and mix well. Spoon the sausage mixture into the baking dish, pour in the egg mixture and top with cheese. Bake for 30 minutes or until eggs are set.

Yield: 6 servings

Twenty-Four-Hour Souffle

2 tablespoons margarine, softened
4 slices bread, crusts removed
2 cups (8 ounces) shredded Cheddar
   cheese

1 teaspoon mustard
$1^1/_2$ teaspoons salt
4 eggs, beaten
$2^1/_2$ cups milk

Spread the margarine over the bread slices and cut the slices into 1-inch pieces. Place half the bread in a greased 2-quart casserole and top with half the cheese. Repeat the layers. Combine the mustard, salt, eggs and milk in a bowl and mix well. Pour the egg mixture into the casserole. Chill, covered, overnight.

Let stand at room temperature for 1 hour before baking. Preheat the gas oven to 325 degrees. Place the casserole in a large pan. Add hot water to a depth of 1 inch. Bake, uncovered, for $1^1/2$ hours or until set.

Yield: 6 servings

Sausage Breakfast Casserole

1 pound bulk pork sausage
6 slices white bread
3 tablespoons margarine, softened
$1^1/_2$ cups (6 ounces) shredded longhorn
   cheese

5 eggs, beaten
2 cups half-and-half
1 teaspoon salt
1 teaspoon dry mustard

Brown the sausage in a skillet over a medium flame, stirring until crumbly; drain and set aside. Spread each slice of the bread with margarine and cut the slices into 1-inch pieces. Place the bread in a greased 9×13-inch baking dish. Cover with the sausage and top with cheese.

Combine the eggs, half-and-half, salt and dry mustard in a bowl and mix well. Pour the egg mixture into the baking dish. Chill, covered, for 8 hours or longer. Let stand at room temperature for several minutes. Preheat the gas oven to 350 degrees. Bake, uncovered, for 40 to 50 minutes or until set and golden.

Yield: 6 servings

Honey-Pecan Fried Chicken

2 (3-pound) chickens, cut up
4 cups buttermilk
1 cup self-rising flour
3/4 teaspoon salt
1/4 teaspoon garlic powder

1/4 teaspoon cayenne pepper
1 cup (2 sticks) margarine
1/2 cup honey
1/2 cup coarsely chopped pecans
Vegetable oil for frying

Rinse the chicken and pat dry. Combine the buttermilk and chicken in a large bowl and chill, covered, for 1 1/2 hours; drain. Combine the flour, salt, garlic powder and cayenne pepper and coat the chicken with the flour mixture, shaking off the excess. Place on a rack and let stand for 20 minutes.

Melt the margarine in a saucepan over a low flame. Add the honey and bring to a boil, stirring frequently. Add the pecans and cook for 15 minutes, stirring frequently. Set the honey glaze aside; keep warm.

Heat 1/2 to 3/4 inch oil in a large heavy skillet over a medium flame. Add the chicken in batches; do not crowd. Fry for 10 minutes on each side or until chicken is crisp, golden brown and cooked through. Drain on paper towels. Arrange the chicken pieces on a serving platter and drizzle with the honey glaze. Serve immediately.

Yield: 6 to 8 servings

Melting Pot Chicken

4 chicken breasts, boned, skinned
3/4 cup salsa

3/4 cup Italian dressing
4 slices mozzarella cheese

Place the chicken breasts in a shallow dish. Pour 1/4 cup of the salsa and 1/4 cup of the Italian dressing over the chicken. Marinate in the refrigerator for 1 to 2 hours. Drain and discard the marinade. Preheat the gas grill or gas broiler. Place the chicken on a grill rack or broiler pan. Grill until cooked through. Top each chicken breast with 1 piece of cheese. Combine the remaining salsa and Italian dressing in a saucepan and bring to a boil, stirring occasionally. Simmer for 1 minute. Pour the sauce over the chicken. Serve over hot cooked pasta or rice or wrapped in a flour tortilla.

Yield: 4 servings

Dill Grilled Chicken

4 chicken leg quarters
1/2 cup (1 stick) margarine
1 teaspoon hickory smoked salt
1/2 teaspoon pepper

1/4 teaspoon garlic powder
2 tablespoons grated Parmesan cheese
1/2 cup lime juice
1 tablespoon dillweed

Place the chicken in a shallow baking dish. Melt the margarine in a saucepan over a low flame. Add the salt, pepper, garlic powder, Parmesan cheese, lime juice and dillweed and bring to a boil, stirring frequently. Cook for 5 minutes. Pour the sauce over the chicken and marinate in the refrigerator for 2 hours, turning occasionally. Drain the chicken.

Preheat the gas grill using a medium-low flame. Place the chicken on the grill. Grill for 45 minutes to 1 hour or until cooked through, turning frequently. May be broiled in a gas oven if desired.

Yield: 4 to 6 servings

Honey Pineapple Chicken Breasts

3/4 cup clover honey
1/2 cup pineapple preserves
2 tablespoons finely chopped fresh
   gingerroot

2 tablespoons finely chopped fresh mint
6 boneless skinless chicken breasts

Preheat the gas grill to medium. Combine the honey, preserves, ginger and mint in a small bowl and mix well. Divide the honey mixture into 2 portions and reserve 1 portion for serving sauce. Place the chicken on the grill. Grill the chicken for 25 minutes or until cooked through, turning and basting occasionally with the remaining honey mixture. Discard any unused basting sauce. Serve the chicken with the reserved honey mixture as a sauce.

Yield: 4 to 6 servings

Chicken and Artichoke Casserole

4 teaspoons margarine
4 ounces fresh mushrooms, sliced
2 boneless skinless chicken breasts, cooked, diced
1 (14-ounce) can whole artichoke hearts, drained, chopped
1 cup sour cream
1/4 cup red wine
1/2 cup (2 ounces) grated Parmesan cheese
1/4 teaspoon salt
Pepper to taste
Paprika to taste

Preheat the gas oven to 375 degrees. Melt the margarine in a skillet over a medium flame. Add the mushrooms and cook for 4 minutes, stirring frequently. Add the chicken and artichokes and mix well. Pour immediately into a greased casserole.

Combine the sour cream, red wine, Parmesan cheese, salt and pepper in a bowl and mix well. Pour the mixture into the casserole and lift the chicken and artichoke pieces to allow the sour cream mixture to flow around the pieces. Sprinkle with paprika. Bake for 25 minutes or until bubbly.

Yield: 4 servings

Energy Saver: *Wash full loads of clothes when possible.*

King Ranch Chicken

1 (3-pound) chicken
1 cup milk
1 (10-ounce) can cream of chicken soup
1 (10-ounce) can cream of mushroom soup
3/4 cup chopped onion
1/2 cup chopped green bell pepper
1 (10-ounce) can diced tomatoes with green chiles
8 ounces fresh mushrooms, sliced (optional)
1 teaspoon chili powder
1 (8-ounce) package tortilla chips
2 cups (8 ounces) shredded sharp Cheddar cheese

Combine the chicken and 5 to 6 cups water in a large pot and boil over a medium flame until tender; drain and reserve the broth for another purpose. Bone and chop the chicken. Discard the skin and bones.

Preheat the gas oven to 350 degrees. Combine the milk and soups in a bowl and mix well. Add the onion, green pepper, tomatoes, mushrooms and chili powder and mix well. Crush the tortilla chips coarsely. Layer the tortilla chips and chicken alternately in a greased 9×13-inch baking dish. Top with the soup mixture and sprinkle with cheese. Bake for 40 minutes or until bubbly.

Yield: 10 to 12 servings

In an effort to keep up with the needs of consumers and the rationing of scarce ingredients, ONG Home Economists created recipes that contributed to the War Effort. Recipes were designed and tested to utilize surplus from the Victory Garden or to make substitutions for rationed ingredients.

Emergency Whipped Cream

2 egg whites
speck of salt
1/2 c. confectioner's sugar
1 t. vanilla
2 t. lemon juice
3 T. very soft butter

Add salt to egg whites and beat until fluffy. Add sugar gradually, beating after each addition to form a meringue. Fold in vanilla and lemon juice. Fold in softened butter. Chill well and serve.

Country Club Hot Chicken Salad

4 cups chopped cooked chicken
2 cups chopped celery
4 hard-cooked eggs, chopped
1 (2-ounce) jar diced pimento, drained
1 tablespoon finely chopped onion
1 cup mayonnaise
2 tablespoons lemon juice
3/4 teaspoon salt
1 cup (4 ounces) shredded Cheddar cheese
2/3 cup sliced almonds, toasted

Preheat the gas oven to 350 degrees. Combine the chicken, celery, eggs, pimento and onion in a large bowl and toss to mix. Blend the mayonnaise, lemon juice and salt in a small bowl. Add the mayonnaise mixture to the chicken mixture and toss to mix and coat. Spoon into a greased 9×13-inch casserole. Bake, covered, for 20 minutes.

Sprinkle with cheese and almonds and bake, uncovered, for 3 minutes longer or until the cheese melts.

Yield: 6 to 8 servings

Energy Saver: When barbecuing chicken or meat on the gas grill, or cooking meat dishes or casseroles in the oven, prepare double or triple recipes and freeze the unused portions for later meals.

Chicken and Wild Rice Casserole

3 pounds chicken pieces
2 cups water
$1/2$ cup dry sherry
1 medium onion, quartered
$1/2$ teaspoon curry powder
2 teaspoons salt
1 rib celery with tops, coarsely chopped
$1/4$ cup ($1/2$ stick) margarine
16 ounces fresh mushrooms, sliced
2 (6-ounce) packages long grain and wild rice mix
3 cups water
1 (10-ounce) can cream of mushroom soup
1 cup sour cream

Combine the chicken, 2 cups water, sherry, onion, curry powder, salt and celery in a large pot over a low flame and cook for 1 hour or until the chicken is tender. Drain the chicken, reserving the broth. Bone the chicken and cut into bite-size pieces; discard the skin and bones.

Melt the margarine in a skillet over a high flame. Add the mushrooms and cook for 4 minutes, stirring frequently; drain. Combine the rice mix, reserved broth and 3 cups water in a medium pot and cook until the rice is tender; do not drain.

Preheat the gas oven to 350 degrees. Add the cream of mushroom soup, sour cream, chicken and mushrooms to the cooked rice and stir gently until well mixed. Pour into a greased 4-quart casserole. Bake for 1 hour.

Yield: 8 to 10 servings

Chicken Divan Crepes

2 (10-ounce) packages frozen broccoli spears with butter sauce
1/4 cup flour
1 (14-ounce) can chicken broth
1/2 cup (2 ounces) shredded Cheddar cheese
1 teaspoon parsley flakes
1/2 teaspoon salt
Dash of onion salt
Dash of pepper
2 tablespoons sour cream
2 tablespoons sherry
1 1/2 cups chopped cooked chicken
1 (2-ounce) can sliced mushrooms, drained
12 frozen, refrigerated or homemade crepes (see page 160)
1/3 cup shredded Cheddar cheese
Grated Parmesan cheese to taste

Prepare the broccoli according to package directions. Drain the butter sauce from the broccoli and reserve. Set the broccoli spears aside. Measure 2 tablespoons of the butter sauce into a saucepan. Add the flour and blend well. Stir in the remaining butter sauce and chicken broth and cook over a medium flame until thickened and smooth, stirring constantly. Add 1/2 cup Cheddar cheese, parsley, salt, onion salt, pepper, sour cream and sherry and cook until the cheese melts, stirring constantly. Add the chicken and mushrooms and mix well.

Preheat the gas oven to 350 degrees. Top each crepe with a broccoli spear and 1 to 2 tablespoons of the chicken mixture. Roll each crepe to enclose the filling. Place seam side up in a greased large shallow baking dish. Top with the remaining chicken mixture and sprinkle with 1/3 cup Cheddar cheese and desired amount of Parmesan cheese. Bake for 20 minutes or until bubbly.

Yield: 6 servings

Chicken and Dumplings

1 (4- to 5-pound) chicken
2 tablespoons salt
1 tablespoon onion powder
2 teaspoons garlic powder
3 quarts water
Dumplings (below)

Combine the chicken, salt, onion powder, garlic powder and water in a large pot. Bring to a boil over a medium flame. Reduce the flame and cook, covered, for 2 hours or until the chicken is tender. Drain, reserve the broth and cool completely. Bone and chop the chicken; discard the skin and bones. Skim the broth and return the chicken pieces and broth to the pot. Bring the chicken and broth mixture to a boil over a medium flame, add the Dumplings several at a time and stir gently. Reduce the flame and cook, covered, for 20 minutes.

Yield: 6 to 8 servings

Dumplings

3 cups flour
1/2 teaspoon salt
1/2 cup shortening
2/3 cup plus 1 tablespoon (about) water

Combine the flour and salt in a mixing bowl. Cut in the shortening until crumbly. Add the water 1 tablespoon at a time until a soft dough forms. Shape into a ball and divide into 4 equal portions. Roll each portion to 1/8-inch thickness on a floured surface and cut into 1×2-inch strips.

Cornish Hens Burgundy

2 (12- to 16-ounce) Cornish game hens
Rice and Almond Stuffing (below)

Vegetable oil
Burgundy Glaze (below)

Thaw the hens in the refrigerator for about 24 hours. Preheat the gas oven to 375 degrees. Stuff the game hens with the Rice and Almond Stuffing, closing the openings with skewers. Lace, truss and brush with vegetable oil and place in a small roaster. Bake, covered, for 30 minutes. Remove the cover from the game hens and bake for 1 hour or until cooked through, basting frequently with Burgundy Glaze. Serve with the reserved Burgundy Glaze.

Yield: 2 to 4 servings

Rice and Almond Stuffing

2 tablespoons margarine
3 tablespoons sliced green onions with tops
1/4 cup slivered almonds, toasted
3 tablespoons snipped fresh parsley

1/2 cup cooked long grain rice
1/8 teaspoon salt
Dash of pepper

Melt the margarine in a large skillet. Add the green onions and cook until tender, stirring frequently. Add the almonds, parsley, rice, salt and pepper and mix well.

Burgundy Glaze

1/2 cup red burgundy
1/2 cup currant jelly
2 tablespoons margarine
1 tablespoon lemon juice

2 teaspoons cornstarch
2 teaspoons Worcestershire sauce
1/2 teaspoon allspice
Salt and pepper to taste

Combine the red burgundy, currant jelly, margarine, lemon juice, cornstarch, Worcestershire sauce, allspice, salt and pepper in a medium saucepan and cook over a medium flame until thickened and bubbly, stirring constantly. Divide the glaze into 2 portions. Reserve 1 portion to serve as a sauce. The remaining glaze is to be used as a basting sauce. Discard any unused basting sauce.

Roasted Turkey with Cognac

1 (21- to 24-pound) frozen turkey
10 fresh sage leaves, or 1 teaspoon dried sage
1/4 cup cognac
1/2 cup (1 stick) margarine, melted

Place the turkey in original wrap on a tray and thaw in the refrigerator for 4 to 5 days. Remove the neck and giblets from the body and neck cavities. Rinse the turkey inside and out and pat dry.

Preheat the gas oven to 325 degrees. Loosen the skin from the turkey but do not tear or remove the skin. Insert sage and cognac under the skin. Fold the neck skin toward the backbone and secure with skewers. Tie legs with cord and lift wing tips up and over the back to tuck under and secure.

Place the turkey breast side up on a rack in a shallow roasting pan and brush with margarine. Insert a meat thermometer into the thickest part of the thigh muscle without touching the bone.

Bake, uncovered, for 5 1/2 to 6 hours or until the thermometer registers 180 to 185 degrees. Let stand for 20 to 30 minutes before carving.

Yield: 16 to 18 servings

Bond Sales Soar When Bing Croons

September 18, 1942. During World War II, ONG answered the nation's call to arms by constructing a 96-mile high-pressure pipeline to serve the increased demand of the war and industrial expansion. ONG experimented with storing natural gas in depleted wells, which led to its first storage fields. In addition, at a war benefit golf party held at Southern Hills Country Club in Tulsa, more than 2,500 attendees opened their hearts and pocketbooks to the tune of $315,125. It was the largest Bing Crosby benefit of its time. ONG President Joseph Bowes set the pace by purchasing a $50,000 war bond. In appreciation to Bowes, Bing Crosby dedicated a recording of himself and Bob Wills singing "San Antonio Rose."

Sour Cream Turkey Enchiladas

2 tablespoons margarine
1/2 cup chopped onion
1 (4-ounce) can mushrooms, drained
1 garlic clove, minced
1 1/2 cups chopped cooked turkey
1 (4-ounce) can green chiles, drained
1 cup sour cream
1 1/2 teaspoons chili powder
1 teaspoon cumin
1/2 teaspoon salt
1/4 teaspoon pepper
Vegetable oil for frying
18 tortillas
4 cups (16 ounces) shredded Cheddar cheese
2 cups sour cream

Preheat the gas oven to 350 degrees. Melt the margarine in a large skillet. Add the onion, mushrooms and garlic and cook until tender but not brown, stirring frequently. Reduce the flame to low and add the turkey, green chiles, 1 cup sour cream, chili powder, cumin, salt and pepper and mix well. Cook until heated through, stirring frequently.

Heat 1/2 inch oil in a medium skillet. Fry each tortilla for 3 seconds or until softened. Drain on paper towels. Spread 1 heaping tablespoon of turkey filling down the center of each tortilla and sprinkle with a small amount of cheese. Roll each tortilla to enclose the filling and place seam side down in a greased 9×13-inch baking dish. Bake for 15 minutes.

Top with 2 cups sour cream and the remaining cheese. Bake for 8 minutes or until bubbly.

Yield: 6 servings

Energy Saver: *Clean the dryer lint screen frequently.*

Turkey Tetrazzini

16 ounces thin spaghetti
3/4 cup (1 1/2 sticks) margarine
3/4 cup flour
2 teaspoons salt
2 drops hot red pepper sauce
Freshly ground pepper to taste
3 cups milk
2 cups turkey broth or chicken broth
4 egg yolks, beaten
1/2 cup heavy cream
1/4 cup sherry
1 (4-ounce) jar whole mushrooms, drained
6 cups chopped cooked turkey
4 cups (16 ounces) shredded sharp Cheddar cheese
Paprika to taste

Cook the spaghetti according to the package directions just until tender; drain, rinse, drain well and set aside.

Melt the margarine in a Dutch oven over a medium flame. Blend in the flour gradually to form a smooth paste. Add the salt, hot red pepper sauce and pepper and mix well. Stir in the milk and broth gradually. Bring the mixture to a boil, stirring constantly. Cook until smooth and slightly thickened, stirring constantly. Combine the egg yolks and cream in a small bowl and beat well to mix. Stir a small amount of the hot broth mixture into the egg mixture; stir the egg mixture into the broth gradually. Add the sherry, mushrooms, turkey and spaghetti and stir gently to mix. Divide the mixture equally among three 8×8-inch foil freezer pans. Sprinkle with cheese and paprika. Cover with waxed paper and seal in heavy foil and freeze. Store in the freezer.

To heat: Unwrap the frozen pans and place in a cold gas oven set to 350 degrees. Turn the oven on and bake for 1 hour or until bubbly.

Yield: 12 to 18 servings

Barbecued Fish

2 pounds (1-inch) halibut, sea bass or rockfish fillets
1/4 cup soy sauce
1/2 cup dry white wine
1 tablespoon lemon juice
1 garlic clove, crushed
1/2 teaspoon ground ginger
1/4 cup vegetable oil
1 tablespoon rosemary
3 tablespoons chopped fresh parsley
3 tablespoons butter
8 ounces fresh mushrooms, sliced

Place the fillets side by side in a shallow dish. Combine the soy sauce, wine, lemon juice, garlic, ginger and oil in a small bowl and whisk to mix well. Pour the marinade over the fish and chill, covered, for 4 hours. Drain well.

Preheat the gas grill to low. Sprinkle the fillets with rosemary and parsley. Skewer the fillets or place inside a hinged wire broiler. Grill for 10 to 15 minutes or until the fish flakes easily, turning once.

Melt the butter in a skillet. Add the mushrooms and cook until tender, stirring frequently. Place the fillets on a serving platter. Pour the mushrooms over the grilled fish and serve immediately.

Yield: 6 to 8 servings

Energy Saver: During hot weather, use heat-producing appliances as little as possible and preferably in the cooler hours of the morning. Plan meals requiring less cooking.

Salmon and Rice Florentine

2 (10-ounce) packages frozen chopped
   spinach
1/4 cup (1/2 stick) margarine
2 tablespoons finely chopped onion
1/4 cup flour
1/2 teaspoon salt
Dash of cayenne pepper

1/2 teaspoon dry mustard
2 cups milk
1 1/2 cups (6 ounces) shredded sharp Cheddar
   cheese
1 (15-ounce) can salmon, drained
2 cups cooked rice

Preheat the gas oven to 400 degrees. Prepare the spinach according to the package directions and drain well. Melt the margarine in a skillet. Add the onion and cook until tender, stirring frequently. Add the flour, salt, cayenne pepper and dry mustard and mix well. Reduce the flame to low and stir in the milk gradually. Cook until the mixture thickens, stirring constantly. Add 1 cup of the cheese and cook until melted, stirring constantly. Remove the cheese sauce from the flame. Break the salmon into chunks. Layer the spinach, salmon and rice in a greased baking dish. Top with the cheese sauce and sprinkle with the remaining cheese. Bake for 20 minutes or until bubbly.

Yield: 6 servings

Crab and Asparagus Casserole

1 (10-ounce) package frozen asparagus
   spears, thawed
1/4 cup (1/2 stick) margarine
2 tablespoons finely chopped onion
2 tablespoons flour
1/8 teaspoon curry powder

1 cup milk
1 (5-ounce) jar sharp cheese spread
1 tablespoon lemon juice
1 (6-ounce) can crab meat, drained, flaked
1/2 cup bread crumbs

Preheat the gas oven to 350 degrees. Place the asparagus in a greased 1-quart casserole and bake, covered, for 10 to 15 minutes or until tender. Melt the margarine in a saucepan. Add the onion and cook until tender. Reduce the flame and add the flour and curry powder, stirring to mix well. Add the milk gradually, stirring constantly. Cook until thickened, stirring constantly. Add the cheese and lemon juice and stir to mix well. Add the crab meat and cook until heated through. Pour the mixture over the asparagus and sprinkle with bread crumbs. Bake uncovered for 30 minutes.

Yield: 6 servings

Shrimp and Artichoke Casserole

2 (9-ounce) packages frozen artichoke hearts, thawed
1¹⁄₂ pounds shrimp, cooked, peeled, deveined
¹⁄₄ cup (¹⁄₂ stick) margarine
12 ounces fresh mushrooms, sliced
2 tablespoons flour

1 pint light cream
¹⁄₄ cup sherry
1 teaspoon Worcestershire sauce
Salt and pepper to taste
¹⁄₄ cup grated Parmesan cheese
Paprika to taste

Preheat the gas oven to 350 degrees. Arrange the artichokes in a greased casserole and top with the shrimp. Melt 2 tablespoons of the margarine in a skillet, add the mushrooms and cook for 4 minutes, stirring frequently. Place the mushrooms on top of the shrimp. Reduce the flame to low and melt the remaining 2 tablespoons margarine in the skillet. Add the flour and blend well. Add the cream gradually and cook until smooth and thickened, stirring constantly. Add the sherry, Worcestershire sauce, salt and pepper and mix well. Pour the sauce into the casserole and sprinkle with cheese and paprika. Bake for 20 to 30 minutes or until bubbly.

Yield: 6 servings

Cajun Shrimp Etoufee

¹⁄₂ cup (1 stick) margarine
1¹⁄₂ cups chopped onion
¹⁄₂ cup chopped green bell pepper
¹⁄₂ cup chopped celery
1 garlic clove, minced
1 tablespoon flour
¹⁄₂ cup water

2 teaspoons tomato paste
1 tablespoon Worcestershire sauce
2 pounds peeled deveined shrimp or crawfish
1 teaspoon salt
¹⁄₂ teaspoon pepper
¹⁄₂ to 1 teaspoon hot red pepper sauce

Melt the margarine in a skillet over a medium flame. Add the onion, green pepper, celery and garlic and cook until tender. Combine the flour and water in a bowl and mix well. Add the tomato paste and Worcestershire sauce and blend well. Add the tomato mixture to the vegetables and cook for 15 minutes, stirring constantly. Add the shrimp, salt and pepper and cook for 15 minutes, stirring occasionally. Add the hot red pepper sauce, mix well and cook for 5 minutes longer. Serve over hot cooked rice.

Yield: 6 servings

Seafood a la King Arthur

1 pack soda crackers
2/3 cup milk
1 tablespoon butter
1 cup chopped celery
1/2 cup chopped green bell pepper
2 tablespoons chopped onion
2 tablespoons chopped pimento
1 (6-ounce) can crab meat, drained, flaked
1 (4-ounce) can shrimp, drained
1/2 cup mayonnaise
1 teaspoon dry mustard
1 teaspoon Worcestershire sauce
Dash of cayenne pepper
Dash of salt
Finely rolled cracker crumbs to taste

Preheat the gas oven to 350 degrees. Crush the crackers coarsely. Combine the coarse cracker crumbs and milk in a small bowl. Let stand for several minutes.

Melt the butter in a saucepan over a medium flame, add the celery, green pepper and onion and cook until tender. Add the cracker mixture and mix well. Add the pimento, crab meat, shrimp, mayonnaise, mustard, Worcestershire sauce, cayenne pepper and salt and mix gently.

Spoon the mixture into 4 seafood baking shells or ramekins and sprinkle with the fine cracker crumbs. Bake for 30 minutes or until lightly browned.

Yield: 4 servings

Energy Saver: *Cook whole meals or several foods at the same time in the oven.*

Construction of the General Office building in Tulsa was begun in 1926, under the ownership of Phillips Petroleum Company and completed in 1928, after the company was purchased by G.L. Ohrstrom's American Natural Gas Holding Company.

Vegetables and Side Dishes

Asparagus Casserole

2 cups cracker crumbs
2 cups (8 ounces) shredded Cheddar cheese
1 (15-ounce) can asparagus tips
1 (10-ounce) can mushroom soup
1/2 cup (1 stick) margarine, melted

Preheat the gas oven to 350 degrees. Combine the cracker crumbs and cheese in a medium bowl and mix well. Drain the asparagus, reserving 1 cup liquid. Combine the reserved liquid and the soup in a large bowl and mix well.

Layer 1/3 of the cracker mixture, 1/2 of the asparagus and 1/2 of the soup mixture in a greased 2-quart casserole. Repeat the layers and top with the remaining cracker mixture. Drizzle with margarine. Bake for 25 minutes or until golden brown.

Yield: 6 to 8 servings

Broccoli and Rice Casserole

1 (10-ounce) package frozen chopped broccoli
1 cup rice, cooked
1 cup chopped celery
1 (8-ounce) jar process cheese spread
1 (10-ounce) can mushroom soup

Preheat the gas oven to 350 degrees. Cook the broccoli according to package directions and drain well. Combine the broccoli, rice and celery in a medium bowl and mix well. Combine the cheese spread and soup in a large bowl and blend well. Add the rice mixture and stir to mix well. Pour the mixture into a greased 9×9-inch baking dish. Bake for 30 minutes.

Yield: 6 to 8 servings

Favorite Baked Beans

3 or 4 bacon slices
2 tablespoons minced onion
1 rib celery, finely chopped
1/4 cup finely chopped green bell pepper
1/4 cup ketchup

2 tablespoons molasses
3 drops Tabasco sauce
2 tablespoons brown sugar
1 (21-ounce) can pork and beans

Preheat the gas oven to 375 degrees. Fry the bacon in a skillet until crisp. Reserve 2 tablespoons of the bacon drippings, drain the bacon and set aside. Combine the bacon drippings, onion, celery and green pepper in the skillet and cook until tender-crisp, stirring frequently. Combine the ketchup, molasses, Tabasco sauce and brown sugar in a large bowl and blend well. Add the pork and beans and onion mixture and mix well. Pour into a greased 1-quart baking dish and top with the bacon slices. Bake for 30 minutes or until bubbly.

Yield: 4 to 6 servings

Spicy Hoppin' John

2 cups dried black-eyed peas
8 cups water
1 medium ham hock
1 (16-ounce) can diced tomatoes
1 cup chopped onion
1 cup chopped celery

1 teaspoon salt
2 teaspoons chili powder
1/4 teaspoon crushed basil
1 bay leaf
1 cup long grain rice

Sort and rinse the peas. Combine the peas and water in a large pot and let stand overnight. (Shortcut the overnight soak by bringing the peas and water to a boil, boil for 2 minutes, remove from the flame and let stand, covered, for 1 hour.) Add the ham hock, tomatoes, onion, celery, salt, chili powder, basil and bay leaf and cook, covered, over a low flame for 1 1/4 hours or until the peas are tender.

Remove the ham hock, shred the ham and discard the bone. Return the ham to the peas, add the rice and simmer, covered, for 20 minutes or until the rice is tender, adding a small amount of water if necessary. Remove the bay leaf before serving.

Yield: 6 to 8 servings

French-Style Green Beans

1 (10-ounce) package frozen French-style
   green beans
1/2 teaspoon salt
1 teaspoon minced onion, or 1/2 teaspoon
   instant minced onion

1 tablespoon margarine
2 tablespoons slivered almonds
1 (4-ounce) can mushrooms, drained
   (optional)

Preheat the gas grill to medium. Place the beans on a large piece of heavy foil. Add the salt, onion, margarine, almonds and mushrooms. Seal the foil with a double fold, leaving room for expansion. Grill for 20 minutes.

Yield: 3 to 4 servings

Request Green Beans

1 (16-ounce) can cut green beans
1 (3-ounce) can French-fried onions
1 (10-ounce) can cream of mushroom soup

1 (4-ounce) can mushrooms
2 tablespoons toasted almonds
1/2 cup (2 ounces) shredded Cheddar cheese

Preheat the gas oven to 375 degrees. Drain the green beans well. Layer the green beans and French-fried onions alternately in a greased casserole until all the ingredients are used.

Combine the soup, mushrooms and almonds in a bowl and mix well. Pour over the green bean and onion layers and sprinkle with cheese. Bake for 30 minutes.

Yield: 4 to 6 servings

Energy Saver: *Preheat the gas grill for 10 minutes; cook several foods at once; turn the flame to low or medium and cook with the cover down whenever possible.*

Broccoli Almondine

1 (10-ounce) package frozen chopped broccoli
1/4 cup (1/2 stick) margarine
1/4 cup finely chopped onion
2 tablespoons flour
1/2 teaspoon salt
1/8 teaspoon pepper
1/2 cup milk
1 (8-ounce) jar cheese spread
2 eggs, beaten
1/2 cup soft bread crumbs
1 tablespoon margarine, melted
1/4 cup toasted slivered almonds

Preheat the gas oven to 325 degrees. Prepare the broccoli according to the package directions and drain well and set aside.

Melt the 1/4 cup margarine in a medium saucepan, add the onion and cook until tender, stirring frequently. Add the flour, salt and pepper and mix well. Add the milk and cook over a low flame until thickened, stirring constantly. Add the cheese and stir until the cheese melts. Stir a small amount of the hot cheese mixture into the eggs; stir the eggs into the cheese mixture. Cook until well mixed, stirring constantly. Add the broccoli and mix well.

Pour into a greased 1 1/2-quart casserole. Combine the bread crumbs and the 1 tablespoon melted margarine in a small bowl and toss to mix well. Sprinkle over the broccoli mixture. Top with almonds. Bake for 40 to 45 minutes or until golden brown. May be prepared and chilled before baking if desired; increase baking time by 5 minutes.

Yield: 8 servings

Brussels Sprouts with Walnut Vinaigrette

4 cups fresh brussels sprouts, or
    2 (10-ounce) packages frozen brussels sprouts
Walnut Vinaigrette (below)
1 cup coarsely chopped walnuts

Cut an X into the bottom of each brussels sprout. Combine the sprouts with enough water to cover in a saucepan and cook over a medium flame until tender-crisp. Drain the brussels sprouts well. Place in a serving bowl. Add the Walnut Vinaigrette and the walnuts; toss to coat well and serve immediately.

Yield: 8 servings

Walnut Vinaigrette

1/4 cup red wine vinegar
3 tablespoons brown sugar
1 tablespoon Dijon mustard
1/2 cup walnut oil or vegetable oil
Pinch of freshly grated nutmeg
Salt and freshly ground pepper to taste

Combine the wine vinegar, brown sugar and Dijon mustard in a large bowl. Add the walnut oil in a fine stream, whisking constantly. Add nutmeg, salt and pepper and mix well.

Energy Saver: When baking a small quantity of food, place it near the center of the oven. For a large amount of food, allow at least one inch of space between pans and oven lining to permit free circulation of heat for even baking.

Maple-Glazed Carrots

2 pounds baby carrots
1/4 cup (1/2 stick) margarine
1/4 cup maple syrup
1/2 cup golden raisins (optional)

Cook the carrots in a large saucepan of salted boiling water until tender; drain and set aside. Melt the margarine in a large skillet over a low flame. Add the maple syrup and mix well. Add the carrots and cook for 5 minutes, turning the carrots constantly to coat well. Add the raisins and cook for 5 minutes or until the carrots are lightly browned and glazed, turning occasionally.

Yield: 8 to 10 servings

Classy Carrots

1 (16-ounce) package frozen crinkle-cut carrots
1/4 cup orange marmalade
2 tablespoons margarine
4 teaspoons orange-flavored liqueur
Salt and pepper to taste

Prepare the carrots according to the package instructions; drain well and set aside. Combine the marmalade, margarine and liqueur in a saucepan and cook over a low flame until well mixed. Add the carrots and cook until the carrots are coated, stirring gently. Season with salt and pepper.

Yield: 4 to 5 servings

In an effort to keep up with the needs of its consumers, the ONG Home Service Department took to the airwaves at the dawn of the television era. "Lookin' at Cookin'" premiered in Tulsa, November 1949. The program evolved into a five-minute format featuring one recipe. The weekday show ran from 1949 to December 1980, making it the longest-running, single-sponsored television program of its time. Its popularity sparked "Foods 'n Focus" in Oklahoma City.

Scalloped Celery

1 (3-pound) bunch celery, rinsed
3/4 cup water
6 tablespoons margarine
1/2 cup plus 1 tablespoon flour
1/4 teaspoon dry mustard
1/2 teaspoon salt
1/8 teaspoon white pepper
3 cups milk
1 (3-ounce) package slivered almonds
1 tablespoon margarine, melted
1 cup stuffing mix
2 tablespoons margarine, melted

Preheat the gas oven to 350 degrees. Slice enough of the celery into 1/2-inch pieces (slice the wide pieces in half) to yield about 5 cups. Place the celery and water in a medium saucepan over a medium flame and cook for 10 minutes or until tender-crisp; drain well and set aside.

Melt 6 tablespoons margarine in a large saucepan over a low flame. Add the flour, dry mustard, salt and pepper and mix well. Add the milk gradually and cook until the sauce thickens, stirring constantly.

Place the almonds on a baking sheet and drizzle with 1 tablespoon melted margarine. Bake for 10 minutes or until toasted. Combine the stuffing mix and 2 tablespoons melted margarine in a bowl and mix well; set aside.

Add the celery to the sauce and mix well. Pour into a greased 2-quart casserole, sprinkle with the almonds and top with the stuffing mixture. Bake for 25 to 30 minutes or until golden brown.

Yield: 8 to 10 servings

Cheesy Corn Bake

2 tablespoons margarine
2 tablespoons flour
1/2 teaspoon salt
1/4 teaspoon pepper
1/4 teaspoon hot red pepper sauce

1/2 cup milk
1/2 cup sour cream
1 (16-ounce) can whole kernel corn, drained
1/2 cup (2 ounces) shredded Swiss cheese
1/2 cup buttered bread crumbs

Preheat the gas oven to 350 degrees. Melt the margarine in a saucepan over a low flame. Add the flour, salt, pepper and hot red pepper sauce, mix well and cook until the mixture is smooth and bubbly, stirring constantly. Remove from the flame and stir in the milk and sour cream. Return to the flame and cook until the sauce thickens, stirring constantly. Add the corn and cheese and mix well.

Spoon the mixture into a lightly greased 1-quart casserole. Sprinkle with the buttered bread crumbs. Bake for 25 to 30 minutes or until bubbly.

Yield: 6 servings

Quick Corn Mazatlan

1 (16-ounce) can whole kernel corn
3 ounces cream cheese, softened
1 (4-ounce) can diced green chiles

1/4 cup sliced green onions
1/4 cup chopped red bell pepper

Drain the corn, reserving 2 tablespoons liquid. Combine the reserved liquid and cream cheese in a saucepan over a low flame and cook until smooth, stirring constantly. Add the green chiles, green onions, red pepper and corn and mix well. Serve hot or cold.

Yield: 4 to 6 servings

Stuffed Peppers Sicilian

3 medium green bell peppers
Salt to taste
Sicilian Ground Beef Stuffing (below)
1 tablespoon grated Parmesan cheese

Preheat the gas oven to 350 degrees. Slice the top one-fourth from each green pepper. Discard the stems and chop the tops and set aside for the Stuffing. Scoop out the seeds and membranes from the green peppers to form shells and set aside. Sprinkle salt inside the green pepper shells.

Spoon the Sicilian Ground Beef Stuffing into the shells and sprinkle with the cheese. Place in a lightly greased baking dish and bake for 35 minutes.

Yield: 3 servings

Sicilian Ground Beef Stuffing

1 tablespoon vegetable oil
Chopped green bell pepper (from green pepper tops)
3 tablespoons finely chopped onion
2 tablespoons finely chopped celery
1 small garlic clove, minced
8 ounces extra-lean ground beef
1/4 cup tomato purée
1/4 teaspoon salt
1/8 teaspoon pepper

Heat the oil in a large skillet over a medium flame. Add the chopped green pepper, onion, celery and garlic and cook until tender, stirring frequently. Add the ground beef and cook until brown and crumbly; drain. Stir in the tomato purée, salt and pepper.

Cheesy Potatoes in Foil

3 large baking potatoes, peeled, sliced
Salt and pepper to taste
4 or 5 crisp-cooked bacon slices, drained,
   crumbled

1 large onion, sliced
2 cups (8 ounces) cubed sharp American
   cheese
1/2 cup (1 stick) margarine, sliced

Preheat the gas grill to low. Place the potatoes on a large sheet of heavy-duty foil and sprinkle with salt, pepper and bacon. Top with the onion, cheese and margarine. Seal the foil with a double fold, leaving room for expansion. Place the foil packet on the grill. Grill for 1 hour or until the potatoes are tender, turning the packet occasionally.

Yield: 4 to 6 servings

Potatoes Romanoff

5 cups (about 6 whole) diced cooked
   potatoes
2 teaspoons salt
2 cups cottage cheese
1 cup sour cream

1/4 cup minced green onions
1 small garlic clove, crushed
1/2 cup (2 ounces) shredded American cheese
Paprika to taste

Preheat the gas oven to 350 degrees. Sprinkle the potatoes with 1 teaspoon of the salt. Combine the cottage cheese, sour cream, green onions, garlic and remaining 1 teaspoon salt in a large bowl and mix well.

Fold in the potatoes and pour into a greased 1 1/2-quart casserole. Top with cheese and sprinkle lightly with paprika. Bake for 40 to 45 minutes or until heated through and lightly browned.

Yield: 6 servings

Red Cabbage with Apples

1 (2- to 2½-pound) head red cabbage
2/3 cup red wine vinegar
2 tablespoons sugar
2 teaspoons salt
2 tablespoons bacon drippings
2 medium apples, peeled, sliced
1/2 cup finely chopped onion
1 onion, peeled
2 cloves
1 small bay leaf
5 cups boiling water
3 tablespoons dry red wine
3 tablespoons red currant jelly (optional)

Shred the cabbage as desired. Combine the cabbage, vinegar, sugar and salt in a large bowl and toss to coat well.

Melt the bacon drippings in a 4- or 5-quart saucepan over a medium flame. Add the apples and chopped onion and cook for 5 minutes or until the apples are lightly browned, stirring frequently.

Stud the peeled onion with the cloves. Add the cabbage, peeled onion, bay leaf and boiling water to the apple mixture, mix gently and bring to a boil, stirring occasionally. Reduce the flame to low and cook, covered, for 1½ to 2 hours or until the cabbage is tender and has absorbed most of the liquid, stirring occasionally.

Remove the peeled onion and bay leaf, add the wine and jelly and mix well.

Yield: 4 to 6 servings

Sweet Potato Balls

2 cups cold mashed sweet potatoes
1 egg, beaten
1/4 cup (1/2 stick) margarine, melted
1/2 teaspoon salt

1/4 teaspoon nutmeg
6 marshmallows
1 1/2 cups cereal flakes, crushed

Preheat the gas oven to 400 degrees. Combine the sweet potatoes, egg, 2 tablespoons of the margarine, salt and nutmeg in a large bowl and mix well.

Divide the mixture into 6 equal portions. Shape each portion into a flat patty and press a marshmallow into each center. Wrap the sweet potatoes around the marshmallows to enclose completely and shape into balls.

Combine the remaining 2 tablespoons margarine and the cereal flakes in a small bowl and mix well. Roll each sweet potato ball in the cereal mixture to coat. Place in a greased baking dish. Bake for 15 minutes. May use freshly cooked or canned sweet potatoes.

Yield: 4 servings

Spinach Casserole

1 (10-ounce) package frozen chopped
    spinach, thawed
8 ounces cream cheese, softened
1 (10-ounce) can cream of mushroom soup

1 (8-ounce) can sliced water chestnuts,
    drained
1 (3-ounce) can French-fried onions

Preheat the gas oven to 350 degrees. Drain the spinach, squeeze dry and set aside. Combine the cream cheese and soup in a saucepan over a low flame and cook until blended, stirring constantly. Combine the soup mixture, spinach, water chestnuts and 2/3 of the French-fried onions in a bowl and mix well. Pour into a greased 1-quart casserole and sprinkle with the remaining onions. Bake for 20 minutes.

Yield: 4 to 6 servings

Curried Fruit

1 (29-ounce) can peach halves
1 (29-ounce) can pear halves
1 (20-ounce) can pineapple chunks
5 maraschino cherries, sliced

1/3 cup margarine, melted
3/4 cup packed brown sugar
2 to 4 teaspoons curry powder

Preheat the gas grill to low. Drain all the fruit well. Place the peaches, pears, pineapple and cherries in a flameproof baking dish or skillet.

Combine the margarine, brown sugar and curry powder in a small bowl, mix well and pour over the fruit mixture. Place the baking dish on the grill. Heat for 20 to 25 minutes or until bubbly. Serve as a side dish with meat or poultry.

Yield: 6 to 8 servings

Grits Souffle

1 1/2 cups grits
6 cups boiling water
2 teaspoons seasoned salt
1 teaspoon onion salt
1 teaspoon garlic salt

3/4 teaspoon Worcestershire sauce
1/2 cup (1 stick) margarine
3 eggs, slightly beaten
8 to 16 ounces longhorn cheese, cubed
Paprika to taste

Cook the grits in the boiling water for 5 minutes according to the package directions. Stir in the seasoned salt, onion salt, garlic salt, Worcestershire sauce and margarine. Stir 2 to 3 tablespoons of the hot grits into the eggs; stir the eggs into the grits. Add the cheese and cook until cheese melts, stirring constantly. Pour into a greased 2-quart soufflé dish and sprinkle generously with paprika. Chill, covered, overnight.

Preheat the gas oven to 350 degrees. Bake for 1 1/2 hours.

Yield: 12 to 16 servings

Tiny Dumplings (Spatzle)

3 cups flour
1/2 teaspoon salt
1/4 teaspoon nutmeg
4 eggs, slightly beaten
1 cup milk
2 quarts water
1/2 teaspoon salt
1/2 cup (1 stick) margarine, melted (optional)
1 cup fine dry bread crumbs (optional)

Combine the flour, 1/2 teaspoon salt and nutmeg in a large bowl and mix well. Add the eggs and mix well; the mixture will be crumbly. Add the milk in a fine stream, mixing until the dough is smooth.

Bring the water and 1/2 teaspoon salt to a boil in a large saucepan over a high flame. Place a large colander, preferably with large holes, over the saucepan and press a few tablespoons of the dough at a time directly into the boiling water; stir gently to separate. Cook for 5 to 8 minutes or until tender, stirring gently. Drain thoroughly in a sieve or colander.

Spatzle are traditionally sprinkled with toasted bread crumbs when served as an accompaniment to roasted meats such as sauerbraten. Melt the margarine in a heavy skillet, add the bread crumbs and cook until golden brown, stirring constantly. Serve the dumplings sprinkled with the toasted bread crumbs.

Yield: 4 to 6 servings

Energy Saver: *Operate the dishwasher only when fully loaded.*

Macaroni and Cheese

2 eggs, beaten slightly
1½ cups milk
2 tablespoons margarine
2 tablespoons flour
Dash of salt

1 cup (4 ounces) shredded American cheese
½ teaspoon Worcestershire sauce
1½ cups cooked elbow macaroni
1 cup lightly buttered soft bread crumbs

Preheat the gas oven to 350 degrees. Combine the eggs and 2 tablespoons of the milk in a small bowl and beat lightly. Melt the margarine in a saucepan over a low flame. Add the flour and salt and blend well. Add the remaining milk gradually and cook until sauce thickens, stirring constantly. Stir a small amount of hot sauce into the eggs; stir the egg mixture into the sauce.

Add the cheese and Worcestershire sauce and mix well. Add the macaroni and mix gently to coat well. Pour into a lightly greased 1-quart casserole and sprinkle with bread crumbs. Bake for 30 minutes.

Yield: 3 to 4 servings

Mexican Rice

3 tablespoons margarine
1 cup uncooked rice
1 small onion, finely chopped
1 beef bouillon cube

1¾ cups hot water
½ cup salsa
1 (4-ounce) can chopped olives, drained
2 tablespoons chopped green onions

Melt the margarine in a saucepan or skillet, add the rice and onion and cook until lightly browned, stirring constantly. Reduce the flame to low, add the bouillon cube, water and salsa and cook, covered, for 30 to 40 minutes or until the rice is tender and the liquid has been absorbed. Stir in the olives and top with the green onions.

Yield: 4 servings

Mushroom Rice Pilaf

1 1/3 cups quick-cooking rice
1 (4-ounce) can sliced mushrooms
1 cup cold water
1/4 cup finely chopped onion

1 teaspoon Worcestershire sauce
1/2 teaspoon salt
3 tablespoons margarine

Preheat the gas grill to medium. Form a pouch with a large piece of heavy foil. Place the rice, undrained mushrooms, water, onion, Worcestershire sauce and salt in the pouch and stir carefully to mix. Dot with 2 tablespoons of the margarine. Fold the edges of the foil to seal pouch tightly, leaving room for expansion. Place on the grill. Cook for 15 to 18 minutes.

Open the pouch carefully and add the remaining 1 tablespoon margarine. Fluff the mixture with a fork before serving.

Yield: 4 servings

Savory Wild Rice

1 (6-ounce) can mushrooms
1/4 cup (1/2 stick) margarine
1/2 cup chopped parsley
1/2 cup chopped green onions
1 cup sliced celery

1 1/4 cups wild rice, rinsed
1 (10-ounce) can consommé
1 teaspoon salt
1/2 teaspoon marjoram

Drain the mushrooms, reserving the liquid. Add enough hot water to the reserved liquid to measure 1 1/2 cups and set aside. Melt the margarine in a saucepan. Add the parsley, onions and celery and cook until tender, stirring constantly. Reduce the flame to low and add the wild rice, consommé, mushroom liquid mixture, salt and marjoram. Cook, covered, for 45 minutes or until the wild rice is tender and the liquid is absorbed.

Add the mushrooms and mix well. Serve as a side dish with poultry or wild game. May substitute long grain rice for wild rice and adjust cooking time as necessary.

Yield: 4 to 6 servings

The Home Service Department Representatives were ambassadors
for the company and made home calls to answer consumers' questions
regarding use and care of natural gas appliances.

Breads

Angel Biscuits

1 envelope dry yeast
2 tablespoons lukewarm water
5 to 5 1/2 cups sifted flour
1 tablespoon baking powder
1 teaspoon baking soda

1 teaspoon salt
1/4 cup sugar
1 cup shortening
2 cups buttermilk

Preheat the gas oven to 400 degrees. Dissolve the yeast in the warm water in a small bowl. Combine the flour, baking powder, baking soda, salt and sugar in a large bowl and mix well. Cut in the shortening until crumbly. Add the yeast and buttermilk and mix well.

Knead on a floured surface until smooth and elastic. Roll the dough to 1/2- to 3/4-inch thickness and cut with a biscuit cutter. Fold the biscuits over and place on a greased baking sheet. Bake for 15 to 20 minutes or until golden brown. May chill or freeze dough or unbaked biscuits for later use.

Yield: 2 1/2 dozen

Apricot and Poppy Seed Swirl

2 (8-count) cans crescent rolls
1/2 cup finely chopped dried apricots
2 tablespoons sugar

2 tablespoons poppy seeds
1/2 cup apricot preserves
1 tablespoon finely chopped almonds

Preheat the gas oven to 375 degrees. Unroll the crescent roll dough. Separate into 4 rectangles, pressing the perforations to seal. Combine the apricots, sugar and poppy seeds and mix well. Spread 1/4 of the mixture over each rectangle and roll as for a jelly roll, sealing the edge and ends.

Wind the dough into a greased 8-inch cake pan, beginning at the outer edge and coiling to the center to form a large spiral. Bake for 20 to 24 minutes or until deep golden brown. Top with the preserves, sprinkle with the almonds and bake for 2 minutes longer. Invert onto a wire rack and cool for 5 minutes. Invert onto a serving plate. Serve warm.

Yield: 1 dozen

Blueberry Kuchen

1 (2-layer) package white cake mix
1 cup packed brown sugar
1 1/3 tablespoons cinnamon
1 teaspoon salt
1/3 cup butter, softened

1 1/3 cups finely crushed cornflakes
1/2 cup chopped pecans
1 (12-ounce) package frozen blueberries, thawed, drained

Preheat the gas oven to 350 degrees. Prepare the cake mix according to the package directions and set the batter aside. Combine the brown sugar, cinnamon, salt and butter in a bowl and mix well. Add the crushed cornflakes and pecans and mix well.

Sprinkle 1 1/2 cups of the cornflake mixture evenly over the bottom of a greased 9×13-inch baking dish. Pour the cake batter into the dish. Top with blueberries and the remainder of the cornflake mixture. Cut through the batter and swirl gently to marbleize. Bake for 40 minutes.

Yield: 12 servings

Sour Cream Coffee Cake

1 cup (2 sticks) margarine, softened
2 cups sugar
2 eggs
1 cup sour cream
1 teaspoon vanilla extract
2 cups sifted flour

1 teaspoon baking powder
1/2 teaspoon salt
1 cup chopped pecans
1/4 cup packed brown sugar
1 teaspoon cinnamon

Preheat the gas oven to 350 degrees. Cream the margarine and sugar in a mixing bowl until light and fluffy. Add the eggs 1 at a time, beating well after each addition. Fold in the sour cream and vanilla extract. Sift the flour, baking powder and salt together. Add the sifted ingredients to the batter and mix well. Pour half the batter into a greased and floured bundt pan.

Combine the pecans, brown sugar and cinnamon and mix well. Sprinkle 3/4 of the pecan mixture over the batter; do not let the pecan mixture touch the side of the pan. Top with the remaining batter and sprinkle with the remaining pecan mixture. Bake for 45 to 60 minutes. Cool in the pan on a wire rack for 10 minutes. Invert onto a serving plate.

Yield: 16 servings

Apple-Filled Pancakes

8 eggs
2 1/2 cups milk
1 cup flour
4 teaspoons sugar

1/2 teaspoon salt
6 tablespoons margarine
Apple Filling (below)
Confectioners' sugar to taste

Preheat the gas broiler. Combine the eggs and milk in a large mixing bowl and whisk just long enough to blend. Combine the flour, sugar and salt and add to the egg mixture several tablespoons at a time, stirring constantly.

Melt 1 tablespoon of the margarine in a heavy ovenproof 10-inch skillet over a medium flame. Pour 1/2 cup of the batter into the skillet, tipping and swirling to coat the bottom. Spread 3/4 cup of the Apple Filling evenly over the batter and cook for 3 minutes.

Pour 1/2 cup of the batter over the apples and place the skillet under the broiler, 6 to 7 inches from the flame. Cook for 2 to 3 minutes or until the top is golden brown and firm. Place the pancake on an individual serving plate and sprinkle with confectioners' sugar. Pancakes may be covered with foil and placed in warm oven until ready to serve.

Yield: 5 to 6 servings

Apple Filling

3 pounds tart cooking apples, peeled
2 tablespoons sugar

1 teaspoon cinnamon
6 tablespoons margarine

Slice the apples into 1/4-inch thick wedges. Combine the sugar and cinnamon and mix well. Melt the margarine in a heavy skillet over a medium flame. Add the apple slices and sprinkle with the sugar mixture. Cook until the apples soften slightly and begin to brown, stirring gently occasionally. Remove from the flame and set aside.

Refrigerator Bran Muffins

3 cups whole bran cereal
1/2 cup hot water
2 cups buttermilk
2 eggs, beaten
3/4 cup shortening
1 cup raisins
21/2 cups sifted flour
1 cup sugar
21/2 teaspoons baking soda
1 teaspoon salt

Preheat the gas oven to 400 degrees. Combine the bran cereal, water and buttermilk in a bowl and mix well. Let stand for 2 minutes or until the liquid is mostly absorbed. Add the eggs and shortening and mix well. Stir in the raisins.

Sift the flour, sugar, baking soda and salt together. Add the flour mixture to the bran mixture, mixing just until combined. Fill greased muffin cups 2/3 full. Bake for 20 minutes or until lightly browned. Serve hot.

Batter may be refrigerated in a covered container for up to 2 weeks; do not stir batter after chilling. If raw eggs are a problem in your area, use an equivalent amount of pasteurized egg substitute.

You may bake all the muffins at one time using paper liners in the muffin cups. Cool the muffins completely, freeze and place in sealable plastic bags to store in the freezer. Reheat in the gas oven or microwave or let stand at room temperature to thaw.

Yield: 21/2 dozen

BLUE STAR HOME

DOORWAY TO QUALITY

ONG Home Service Representatives answered phone calls, tested recipes, prepared media kits, and promoted healthy lifestyles. They held cooking schools, but their primary focus was high school and college home economics classrooms. Each year, ONG demonstrated the benefits of natural gas to future consumers, stressing the comfort, efficiency, and latest technology of a home equipped with natural gas appliances. The education process extended to the new home market, where ONG promoted natural gas homes to potential homebuyers as they viewed model homes.

Princess Gingerbread Muffins

2 cups flour
1 teaspoon baking soda
1/2 teaspoon baking powder
2 teaspoons ginger
1/4 teaspoon allspice
1/4 teaspoon cinnamon
1/2 cup shortening
1/2 cup sugar
2 eggs
1/2 cup molasses
1/2 cup buttermilk

Preheat the gas oven to 375 degrees. Combine the flour, baking soda, baking powder, ginger, allspice and cinnamon and mix well. Set aside. Cream the shortening and sugar in a mixing bowl until light and fluffy.

Add the eggs 1 at a time, beating well after each addition. Stir in the molasses. Add the buttermilk and mix well. Add the flour mixture and mix thoroughly. Fill greased muffin cups 2/3 full.

Bake for 25 to 30 minutes or until golden brown. Batter may be refrigerated in a covered container for several days.

Yield: 2 dozen

Energy Saver: Set the thermostat at the lowest comfortable temperature in winter and the highest comfortable temperature in summer.

Streusel-Topped Orange Muffins

2 cups baking mix
1/4 cup sugar
1 egg, beaten
1/2 cup orange juice
2 tablespoons oil
1/2 cup orange marmalade

1/2 cup chopped pecans
3 tablespoons sugar
1 tablespoon flour
1/2 teaspoon cinnamon
1/4 teaspoon nutmeg
Orange-Pecan Butter (below)

Preheat the gas oven to 400 degrees. Combine the baking mix and 1/4 cup sugar in a large bowl and mix well. Make a well in the center of the mixture.

Combine the egg, orange juice and oil in a small bowl and mix well. Pour the orange juice mixture into the well and stir just until moistened.

Add the marmalade and pecans and mix gently. Fill greased muffin cups 2/3 full. Combine 3 tablespoons sugar, flour, cinnamon and nutmeg and mix well. Sprinkle each muffin with 1 teaspoon of the sugar mixture.

Bake for 18 to 20 minutes or until golden brown. Serve with Orange-Pecan Butter.

Yield: 1 dozen

Orange-Pecan Butter

1/2 cup (1 stick) margarine, softened
1 tablespoon sifted confectioners' sugar

1 tablespoon orange juice
3 tablespoons toasted finely chopped pecans

Cream the margarine and confectioners" sugar in a small bowl until light and fluffy. Add the orange juice and blend well. Stir in the pecans. Chill, covered, until ready to serve.

Yield: 1/2 cup

Jalapeno Corn Bread

3 cups corn bread mix
2 1/2 cups milk
1/2 cup vegetable oil
3 eggs, beaten
2 tablespoons sugar
1 large onion, grated
1 cup cream-style corn

1/2 cup finely chopped fresh or canned
 jalapeño peppers
1 1/2 cups (6 ounces) shredded sharp Cheddar
 cheese
4 ounces crisp-cooked bacon, crumbled
1/4 cup chopped pimentos
1/2 garlic clove, crushed

Preheat the gas oven to 400 degrees. Combine the corn bread mix and milk in a bowl and mix well. Add the oil, eggs and sugar and mix well. Add the onion, corn, jalapeños, cheese, bacon, pimentos and garlic 1 or 2 ingredients at a time, mixing well after each addition. Pour into 3 greased 8×8-inch pans. Bake for 35 minutes or until the corn bread tests done. Serve with vegetables or as a base for chili. May be frozen wrapped in plastic wrap or heavy foil.

Yield: 27 servings

Three-C Bread

2 1/2 cups flour
1 cup sugar
1 teaspoon baking powder
1 teaspoon baking soda
1/2 teaspoon salt
1 teaspoon cinnamon
1/2 cup milk

1/2 cup vegetable oil
3 eggs, beaten
1 (3-ounce) can flaked coconut
1/2 cup chopped maraschino cherries
2 cups shredded carrots
1/2 cup chopped pecans
1/2 cup raisins (optional)

Preheat the gas oven to 350 degrees. Combine the flour, sugar, baking powder, baking soda, salt and cinnamon in a large bowl and mix well. Make a well in the center of the dry ingredients.

Combine the milk, oil and eggs in a medium bowl and mix well. Pour the milk mixture into the well, stirring just until moistened. Stir in the coconut, cherries, carrots, pecans and raisins. Spoon the batter into 3 greased 3×7-inch loaf pans. Bake for 30 to 35 minutes or until a wooden pick inserted in center comes out clean.

Yield: 3 loaves

Irish Soda Bread

4 cups flour
1/4 cup sugar
1 teaspoon salt
1 teaspoon baking powder
2 tablespoons caraway seeds
1/4 cup (1/2 stick) butter or margarine, softened
2 cups raisins
1 1/3 cups buttermilk
1 egg, beaten
1 teaspoon baking soda
1 egg yolk, beaten

Preheat the gas oven to 375 degrees. Sift the flour, sugar, salt and baking powder together in a large bowl. Add the caraway seeds and mix well. Cut in the butter until crumbly. Add the raisins.

Combine the buttermilk, egg and baking soda in a small bowl and mix well. Pour into the flour mixture and mix just until moistened.

Knead on a lightly floured surface until smooth and elastic. Shape into a ball and place in a greased 2-quart casserole. Cut a 1/4-inch deep 4-inch cross in the center and brush with egg yolk. Tradition says this cross keeps leprechauns away.

Bake for 1 hour and 10 minutes or until golden brown and the bread tests done. Cool completely before slicing.

Yield: 1 loaf

Energy Saver: Plan oven, broiler, or skillet meals that use one burner when possible.

Glazed Lemon-Walnut Bread

1/4 cup (1/2 stick) margarine, softened
3/4 cup sugar
2 eggs
2 cups flour
2 1/2 teaspoons baking powder
1 teaspoon salt

3/4 cup milk
2 teaspoons grated lemon zest
1/2 cup finely chopped walnuts
1/4 cup plus 1 tablespoon sifted
   confectioners' sugar
1 teaspoon lemon juice

Preheat the gas oven to 350 degrees. Cream the margarine and sugar in a mixing bowl until light and fluffy. Add the eggs 1 at a time, beating well after each addition. Combine the flour, baking powder and salt. Add to the margarine mixture alternately with the milk, mixing well after each addition and ending with the flour mixture. Stir in the lemon zest and walnuts. Pour the batter into a greased 5×9-inch loaf pan. Bake for 45 to 50 minutes or until the loaf tests done.

Cool in the pan for 10 minutes. Remove to a wire rack to cool completely. Combine the confectioners' sugar and lemon juice in a small bowl, stirring until smooth. Drizzle the lemon glaze over the loaf.

Yield: 1 loaf

Pumpkin Bread

2/3 cup shortening
2 2/3 cups sugar
4 eggs, beaten
2 cups pumpkin
2/3 cup water
3 1/3 cups flour

1/2 teaspoon baking powder
2 teaspoons baking soda
1/2 teaspoon ground cloves
2/3 cup chopped pecans
2/3 cup chopped dates (optional)

Preheat the gas oven to 350 degrees. Cream the shortening and sugar in a mixing bowl until light and fluffy. Add the eggs, pumpkin and water and mix well. Sift the flour, baking powder, baking soda and ground cloves together and stir into the pumpkin mixture. Fold in the pecans and dates. Pour into 3 greased 5×9-inch loaf pans. Bake for 50 to 55 minutes or until a wooden pick inserted in center comes out clean. Cool in pans for 10 minutes. Turn onto wire racks to cool completely.

Yield: 3 loaves

Grilled Cheese Bread

1 French baguette
3 ounces cream cheese, softened
1/2 cup (2 ounces) shredded Cheddar cheese
2 tablespoons toasted sesame seeds

2 tablespoons chopped green onion
1 to 2 tablespoons milk
2 teaspoons Dijon mustard

Preheat the gas grill to medium. Cut the bread into 1-inch slices, cutting to but not through the bottom of the loaf.

Combine the cream cheese, Cheddar cheese, sesame seeds, green onion, milk and Dijon mustard in a bowl, mix well and spread between the slices of bread. Wrap the baguette loosely in foil. Place on the grill. Grill for 20 minutes, turning once.

Yield: 12 servings

Bubble Bread

18 frozen dinner rolls
1 cup packed brown sugar
1 (3-ounce) package butterscotch cook-and-
    serve pudding mix

1/4 cup sugar
1 teaspoon cinnamon
1/2 cup chopped pecans
1/2 cup (1 stick) butter, melted

Arrange the frozen rolls in a greased and floured bundt pan. Combine the brown sugar, pudding mix, sugar, cinnamon and pecans in a small bowl, mix well and sprinkle over the rolls. Drizzle with the melted butter.

Let stand at room temperature, loosely covered, overnight. Preheat the gas oven to 350 degrees. Bake for 30 minutes or until the rolls are golden brown. Invert onto a serving plate and serve warm.

Yield: 18 servings

Herbed Parmesan Bread

2 envelopes dry yeast
2 cups warm water
2 tablespoons sugar
2 teaspoons salt

2 tablespoons margarine, softened
1/2 cup plus 1 tablespoon Parmesan cheese
1 1/2 tablespoons oregano
4 1/4 cups flour

Dissolve the yeast in the water in a large mixing bowl. Add the sugar, salt, margarine, 1/2 cup of the cheese, oregano and 3 cups of the flour and beat at low speed until moistened. Beat at medium speed for 2 minutes or until smooth. Add the remaining 1 1/2 cups flour gradually, beating with a slotted spoon. Place in a greased bowl, turning to coat the surface. Let rise, covered, in a warm place for 45 minutes. Preheat the gas oven to 375 degrees. Stir the batter with a wooden spoon for 25 strokes. Place the dough in a greased 2-quart casserole and sprinkle with the remaining 1 tablespoon cheese. Bake for 55 minutes.

Yield: 12 servings

Honey Whole Wheat Bread

4 cups whole wheat flour
1/2 cup nonfat dry milk powder
1 tablespoon salt
2 envelopes dry yeast

3 cups water
1/2 cup honey
2 tablespoons vegetable oil
3 1/2 to 4 cups flour

Combine 3 cups of the whole wheat flour, milk powder, salt and yeast in a mixing bowl and mix well. Combine the water, honey and oil in a saucepan and heat until warm, 115 to 120 degrees. Add to the whole wheat flour mixture and beat at low speed for 30 seconds, scraping the sides of the bowl constantly. Beat at medium speed for 3 minutes. Add the remaining 1 cup whole wheat flour gradually, beating constantly. Add enough flour to form a moderately stiff dough.

Knead on a floured surface until smooth and elastic. Place in a greased bowl, turning to coat the surface. Let rise, covered, in a warm place for 45 to 60 minutes or until doubled in bulk. Punch the dough down and divide into halves. Let rest, covered, for 10 minutes. Shape into loaves and place in greased 5×9-inch loaf pans. Let rise, covered, in a warm place for 30 to 45 minutes or until doubled in bulk. Preheat the gas oven to 375 degrees. Bake for 30 to 35 minutes or until bread tests done.

Yield: 2 loaves

English Muffin Loaves

2 tablespoons (about) cornmeal
3 cups flour
2 envelopes dry yeast
1 tablespoon sugar
2 teaspoons salt
1/4 teaspoon baking soda
2 cups milk
1/2 cup water
3 cups flour

Grease two 5×9-inch loaf pans. Sprinkle lightly with cornmeal and set aside. Combine 3 cups flour, yeast, sugar, salt and baking soda in a large bowl and mix well. Combine the milk and water in a saucepan and heat until very warm, 120 to 130 degrees. Add the warm milk to the dry ingredients and mix well.

Stir in 3 cups flour to form a stiff batter. Spoon into the prepared loaf pans. Sprinkle the batter with additional cornmeal. Let rise, covered, in a warm place for 45 minutes.

Preheat the gas oven to 400 degrees. Bake for 25 minutes. Cool in pans for 5 minutes. Remove to wire racks to cool completely. Slice, toast and serve.

Yield: 2 loaves

ONG began sending recipes to customers' homes in the summer of 1970, when "Flame Tips" was born. Previously, billing information was sent on postcards, but a customer newsletter became possible with the advent of envelope billing. The monthly recipe has always been a favorite section of "Flame Tips" readers, and more than 400 recipes have been sent to customers' homes through the newsletter.

Hot Cross Buns

4 to 5 cups flour
1/3 cup sugar
1/2 teaspoon salt
1 1/4 teaspoons cinnamon
1 envelope dry yeast
1 cup milk

1/4 cup (1/2 stick) margarine
2 eggs at room temperature
3/4 cup seedless raisins
1 egg yolk
2 tablespoons cold water
Confectioners' Sugar Frosting (below)

Combine 1 1/4 cups of the flour, sugar, salt, cinnamon and yeast in a large bowl. Combine the milk and margarine in a saucepan and heat over a low flame until warmed. (Margarine does not need to melt.) Add the milk mixture to the dry ingredients gradually and beat at medium speed for 2 minutes, scraping the sides of the bowl occasionally. Add the eggs and 1/2 cup of the flour or enough to form a thick batter. Beat at high speed for 2 minutes, scraping the sides of the bowl occasionally.

Stir in enough of the remaining flour to make a soft dough. Knead on a floured surface for 8 to 10 minutes or until smooth and elastic. Place in a greased bowl, turning to coat the surface. Let rise, covered, in a warm place for 1 hour or until doubled in bulk. Punch the dough down, turn on a lightly floured surface and knead in the raisins. Divide the dough into 18 equal pieces and shape each piece into a ball. Divide the balls evenly between 2 greased 8-inch baking dishes.

Combine the egg yolk and water in a small bowl, mix well and brush over the dough balls. Let rise, covered, in a warm place for 1 hour or until doubled in bulk. Preheat the gas oven to 375 degrees. Cut a cross into the top of each dough ball with a sharp knife. Bake for 20 to 25 minutes or until golden brown. Remove to wire racks to cool. Pipe the Confectioners' Sugar Frosting on the buns to form crosses (X).

Yield: 1 1/2 dozen

Confectioners' Sugar Frosting

3/4 cup confectioners' sugar
1/2 teaspoon vanilla extract
1 tablespoon milk or cream

Combine the confectioners' sugar, vanilla and milk in small bowl and mix until smooth.

Best Ever Rolls

1 envelope dry yeast
1/2 cup warm water
3/4 cup hot water
1 1/4 cups milk
1/4 cup instant mashed potato granules
2/3 cup margarine, softened

1/2 cup sugar
1 1/2 teaspoons salt
2 eggs, beaten
6 to 7 cups flour
Margarine, melted

Dissolve the yeast in 1/2 cup warm water. Combine 3/4 cup hot water and 1/4 cup of the milk in a saucepan and bring to a boil, stirring frequently. Pour into a mixing bowl and beat in the potato granules. Warm the remaining 1 cup milk and pour over the potato mixture. Add the margarine, sugar and salt and mix well. Let stand until cooled to lukewarm. Add the yeast, eggs and 3 cups of the flour and beat until smooth and light. Stir in enough flour to make a firm dough. Knead on a floured surface for 10 minutes or until smooth and elastic. Place in a greased bowl, turning to coat the surface. Chill, covered, until ready to use. Shape into rolls and arrange on a greased baking sheet. Brush with melted margarine and let rise in a warm place for 1 hour or until doubled in bulk. Preheat the gas oven to 400 degrees. Bake for 15 to 20 minutes or until golden brown. Refrigeration is not required before shaping into rolls.

Yield: 3 1/2 dozen

Refrigerator Rolls

1 envelope dry yeast
2 tablespoons lukewarm water
1 cup milk, scalded
1/2 cup sugar
1 1/2 teaspoons salt

1/2 teaspoon mace (optional)
1 teaspoon grated lemon zest (optional)
2 eggs, or 4 egg yolks, beaten
4 cups sifted flour
1/2 cup melted shortening

Dissolve the yeast in the warm water in a small bowl. Combine the milk, sugar, salt, mace and lemon zest in a bowl and mix well. Cool to lukewarm. Add the yeast and eggs and mix well. Add 2 cups of the flour and mix well. Add the melted shortening and beat vigorously. Add the remaining flour gradually, mixing well after each addition; do not knead. Place in a greased bowl, turning to coat the surface. Chill, covered, for several hours. Shape the dough into rolls. Arrange on a greased baking sheet. Let rise in a warm place until doubled in bulk. Preheat the gas oven to 400 degrees. Bake for 12 to 15 minutes or until golden brown.

Yield: 2 dozen

Orange-Cinnamon Rolls

1 envelope dry yeast
3/4 cup warm water
2 1/2 cups baking mix
Orange-Cinnamon Syrup (below)

Dissolve the yeast in the warm water in a large mixing bowl. Stir in the baking mix gradually and beat vigorously. Knead the dough on a lightly floured surface for 20 strokes or until smooth and elastic. Roll into an 8×16-inch rectangle and spread 2/3 of the cooled Orange-Cinnamon Syrup over the dough to within 1/2 inch of the edges. Roll as for a jelly roll, sealing the edge and ends. Cut into 1-inch slices.

Spoon the remaining syrup into greased muffin cups and top with dough slices. Let rise, covered, in a warm place until doubled in bulk.

Preheat the gas oven to 350 degrees. Bake for 25 to 30 minutes or until golden brown.

Yield: 1 dozen

Orange-Cinnamon Syrup

1 cup sugar
2 teaspoons cinnamon
2 tablespoons grated orange zest
1/4 cup (1/2 stick) margarine
3 tablespoons orange juice

Combine the sugar, cinnamon, orange zest, margarine and orange juice in a saucepan and bring to a boil over a medium flame, stirring constantly. Cook for 2 minutes and set aside to cool.

Kolache

1 envelope dry yeast, or 1 cake yeast
3/4 cup warm water
2 tablespoons sugar
2 tablespoons butter, melted
2 1/2 cups baking mix
Cherry preserves
Confectioners' sugar

Dissolve the yeast in the water in a large mixing bowl. Add the sugar, butter and baking mix and beat vigorously for 2 to 3 minutes. Knead on a floured surface for 25 strokes or until smooth and elastic.

Divide into 12 equal portions. Shape into 2-inch balls. Space the balls 3 inches apart on a greased baking sheet. Flatten slightly and make a deep indentation in each center. Fill the indentation with preserves. Let rise in a warm place for 1 to 1 1/2 hours or until doubled in bulk.

Preheat the gas oven to 400 degrees. Bake for 10 minutes or until buns test done. Dust with confectioners' sugar. Serve warm.

Yield: 1 dozen

The first home demonstration floor staged by Oklahoma Natural Gas'
newly created Home Service Department was built in Oklahoma City in 1932.

Cookies and Candies

Apricot Squares

3/4 cup (1 1/2 sticks) margarine, softened
1 cup sugar
2 cups flour
1/2 teaspoon salt
1/2 teaspoon baking soda
1 (3-ounce) can flaked coconut
1/2 cup chopped pecans or walnuts
Apricot Filling (below)

Preheat the gas oven to 350 degrees. Cream the margarine and sugar in a bowl until light and fluffy. Combine the flour, salt and baking soda, mix well and add to the creamed mixture gradually, mixing until crumbly. Stir in the coconut and pecans. Pat 3/4 of the mixture into an ungreased 9×13-inch baking pan. Bake for 10 minutes.

Spread the Apricot Filling evenly over the crust and sprinkle with the remaining coconut mixture. Bake for 30 minutes. Let stand until cool. Cut into 2-inch squares.

Yield: 2 dozen

Apricot Filling

2 (6-ounce) packages dried apricots
3/4 cup sugar

Combine the apricots with enough water to cover in a saucepan and cook over a low flame for 15 minutes or until tender. Drain, reserving 1/4 cup of the liquid.

Chop the apricots coarsely and set aside. Combine the reserved liquid and sugar in a saucepan and cook over a low flame for 5 minutes. Stir in the apricots.

Lunchbox Brownies

1 1/2 cups (3 sticks) margarine, softened
3 cups sugar
6 eggs
1 tablespoon vanilla extract

2 1/2 cups flour
3/4 cup baking cocoa
1 teaspoon salt
1 1/2 cups chopped nuts

Preheat the gas oven to 350 degrees. Cream the margarine and sugar in a bowl until light and fluffy. Add the eggs 1 at a time, beating well after each addition. Add the vanilla extract and mix well. Combine the flour, baking cocoa and salt, add to the creamed mixture and mix well. Stir in the chopped nuts. Spoon the mixture into a greased 9×13-inch baking pan and spread evenly. Bake for 45 minutes or until brownies pull from the sides of the pan. Let stand for 1 hour. Cut into squares.

Yield: 2 to 3 dozen

Brown Sugar Butter Bars

3/4 cup (1 1/2 sticks) butter, softened
1/2 cup sugar
2 cups sifted flour
1/4 teaspoon salt
1/2 teaspoon vanilla extract

1/4 cup (1/2 stick) butter, softened
3 ounces cream cheese, softened
3/4 cup packed brown sugar
1 cup chopped walnuts

Preheat the gas oven to 375 degrees. Combine 3/4 cup butter, sugar, flour, salt and vanilla extract in a mixing bowl and beat at low speed until crumbly. Reserve 1 cup of the mixture and press the remaining mixture into an ungreased 9×13-inch baking pan. Bake for 5 minutes.

Cream 1/4 cup butter, cream cheese and brown sugar in a bowl until light and fluffy. Stir in the walnuts, spread over the baked crust and sprinkle with the reserved flour mixture. Bake for 25 to 30 minutes or until golden. Cool in the pan on a wire rack. Cut into 1 1/2×3-inch bars.

Yield: 2 dozen

German Chocolate Caramel Cookies

1 (2-layer) package German chocolate cake mix
3/4 cup (1 1/2 sticks) margarine, melted
1/3 cup evaporated milk
1 cup chopped nuts
1 cup semisweet chocolate chips
Caramel Filling (below)

Preheat the gas oven to 350 degrees. Combine the cake mix, margarine, evaporated milk and nuts in a bowl and mix until crumbly. Press half the mixture into a greased and floured 9×13-inch baking pan. Bake for 8 minutes.

Sprinkle the chocolate chips over the baked crust and spread with the Caramel Filling. Crumble the remaining cake mix mixture and sprinkle on top. Bake for 18 to 20 minutes.

Cool slightly and chill, covered, for 30 minutes to set the caramel layer. Cut into bars.

Yield: 3 dozen

Caramel Filling

60 light caramels
1/2 cup evaporated milk

Unwrap the caramels and combine with the evaporated milk in a heavy saucepan. Cook over a low flame until the caramels melt, stirring constantly.

Energy Saver: *Preheat the oven 10 minutes or less for baking. Eliminate preheating for cooking meats and most casseroles.*

Hello Dolly Cookies

1/2 cup (1 stick) margarine
1 cup vanilla wafer crumbs
1 cup chocolate chips

1 (3-ounce) can flaked coconut
1 cup coarsely chopped pecans
1 (14-ounce) can sweetened condensed milk

Preheat the gas oven to 325 degrees. Place the margarine in a 9×13-inch baking dish and place in the oven to melt. Layer the vanilla wafer crumbs, chocolate chips, coconut and pecans in the baking dish. Pour the sweetened condensed milk evenly over the layers. Bake for 30 minutes. Let stand until cool. Chill, covered, overnight. Cut into squares.

Yield: 2 dozen

Luscious Lemon Bars

2 cups sifted flour
1/2 cup sifted confectioners' sugar
1 cup (2 sticks) margarine, softened
4 eggs, beaten

2 cups sugar
1/3 cup lemon juice
1/4 cup flour
1/2 teaspoon baking powder

Preheat the gas oven to 350 degrees. Sift 2 cups flour and the confectioners' sugar together into a bowl. Cut in the margarine until crumbly. Press into a greased 9×13-inch baking pan. Bake for 20 to 25 minutes or until lightly browned.

Combine the eggs, sugar and lemon juice in a mixing bowl and mix well. Sift 1/4 cup flour and baking powder together and stir into the lemon juice mixture. Pour over the baked crust. Bake for 25 minutes. Sprinkle with confectioners' sugar. Let stand until cool. Cut into bars.

Yield: 2 1/2 dozen

Pecan Pie Surprise Bars

1 (2-layer) package yellow cake mix
1/2 cup (1 stick) margarine, softened
1 egg, beaten
1/2 cup packed brown sugar

1 1/2 cups dark corn syrup
1 teaspoon vanilla extract
3 eggs, beaten
1 cup chopped pecans

Preheat the gas oven to 350 degrees. Reserve 2/3 cup of the cake mix for the filling. Combine the remaining cake mix, margarine and 1 egg in a medium bowl and mix until crumbly. Press into a greased 9×13-inch baking pan. Bake for 10 to 15 minutes or until light golden brown.

Combine the reserved cake mix, brown sugar, corn syrup, vanilla extract and 3 eggs in a large bowl and beat for 1 to 2 minutes. Pour over the baked layer and sprinkle with pecans. Bake for 25 to 30 minutes or until set. Let stand until cool. Cut into bars.

Yield: 3 dozen

Toffee Bars

1 cup (2 sticks) margarine, softened
1 cup packed brown sugar
1 egg
1 teaspoon vanilla extract

2 cups flour
1 cup chocolate chips
1/2 cup chopped nuts

Preheat the gas oven to 350 degrees. Cream the margarine and brown sugar in a bowl until light and fluffy. Add the egg and vanilla and mix well. Stir in the flour. Spread evenly into 2 greased 8×8-inch baking pans. Bake for 15 minutes.

Sprinkle with chocolate chips; let stand for several minutes to melt slightly. Spread the melted chocolate evenly over the top. Sprinkle with nuts. Let stand until cool. Cut into bars.

Yield: 2 dozen

Chinese Almond Cookies

2 1/2 cups flour
1 teaspoon baking powder
1/4 teaspoon salt
1 egg
3/4 cup sugar
2/3 cup vegetable oil
1 tablespoon orange juice
2 teaspoons almond extract
1 teaspoon vanilla extract
1 egg
1 tablespoon water
1/3 cup blanched almonds

Preheat the gas oven to 350 degrees. Mix the flour, baking powder and salt together and set aside. Place 1 egg in a large bowl and add the sugar gradually, beating constantly. Combine the oil, orange juice, almond extract and vanilla extract in a medium bowl and mix well. Add to the egg mixture gradually, beating constantly.

Add half the dry ingredients and beat until well mixed. Fold in the remaining dry ingredients. Knead lightly on a lightly floured surface until smooth. Shape into 1-inch balls, arrange on a greased cookie sheet and flatten with a fork.

Beat 1 egg and water in a small bowl. Brush the egg wash lightly on the cookies. Place an almond in the center of each.

Bake for 12 minutes. Cool on the cookie sheet for 1 minute and remove to wire racks to cool completely.

Yield: 3 dozen

White Chocolate Macadamia Cookies

1/2 cup (1 stick) margarine, softened
1/2 cup packed brown sugar
1 egg
2 teaspoons vanilla extract

1 cup plus 2 tablespoons flour
1/2 teaspoon baking soda
8 ounces white chocolate, coarsely chopped
1 (3-ounce) jar macadamia nuts, chopped

Cream the margarine and brown sugar in a bowl until light and fluffy. Add the egg and vanilla extract and beat well. Combine the flour and baking soda, add to the creamed mixture and mix well. Stir in the white chocolate and macadamia nuts. Chill, covered, for several hours.

Preheat the gas oven to 350 degrees. Shape the cookie dough into 1-inch balls and place 2 inches apart on an ungreased cookie sheet. Bake for 8 to 10 minutes or until lightly browned. Cool on the cookie sheet for 1 minute and remove to wire racks to cool completely.

Yield: 4 dozen

Chocolate Crinkles

1/2 cup shortening
1 2/3 cups sugar
2 teaspoons vanilla extract
2 eggs, beaten
6 tablespoons baking cocoa
2 cups flour

2 teaspoons baking powder
1/2 teaspoon salt
1/3 cup milk
1/2 cup nuts
Confectioners' sugar

Cream the shortening and sugar in a bowl until light and fluffy. Add the vanilla extract and eggs and beat well. Sift the baking cocoa, flour, baking powder and salt together and add to the creamed mixture alternately with the milk, mixing well after each addition. Stir in the nuts. Chill, covered, for 3 hours or longer.

Preheat the gas oven to 350 degrees. Shape into small balls and roll in confectioners' sugar to coat. Place 2 inches apart on greased cookie sheets. Bake for 10 to 12 minutes. Cool on a cookie sheet for 1 minute and remove to wire racks to cool completely.

Yield: 2 dozen

Chocolate Lovers' Cookies

2 cups flour
1 teaspoon baking soda
3/4 teaspoon salt
1 cup (2 sticks) margarine, softened
3/4 cup packed dark brown sugar
1/2 cup sugar
1 teaspoon vanilla extract
1 egg
1/4 cup sour cream
1 1/3 cups German's sweet chocolate chips
1 cup coarsely chopped nuts

Preheat the gas oven to 375 degrees. Combine the flour, baking soda and salt. Cream the margarine, brown sugar and sugar in a bowl until light and fluffy. Add the vanilla extract, egg and sour cream and mix well. Add the flour mixture gradually, beating until smooth. Stir in the chocolate chips and nuts.

Drop by scant 1/4 cupfuls 2 inches apart onto an ungreased cookie sheet. Bake for 12 minutes or until lightly browned. Cool on the cookie sheet for 1 minute and remove to wire racks to cool completely.

Yield: 2 dozen

We're Working For Your Energy Future

In the early 1970s phrases such as "energy crisis" and "energy crunch" were on everybody's mind. People looked to Oklahoma, the third-ranked natural gas producer in the continental United States, for hope in an uncertain energy situation. Eyes began to focus on the Anadarko Basin of Western Oklahoma with its potential of 30 trillion cubic feet of gas in a 12,000-square-mile region. By 1981 ONG had laid 515 miles of pipeline and participated in drilling 90 wells to supply the energy demands of the nation.

Fruitcake Cookies

1 1/2 teaspoons baking soda
1 1/2 teaspoons milk
1/4 cup (1/2 stick) margarine, softened
1 cup packed brown sugar
2 eggs, beaten
1 1/2 cups sifted flour
1/4 teaspoon ground cloves
1/2 teaspoon nutmeg
1/2 teaspoon cinnamon
8 ounces candied cherries
8 ounces candied pineapple, chopped
16 ounces golden raisins
1/2 cup bourbon or apple juice
16 ounces pecan halves

Preheat the gas oven to 300 degrees. Dissolve the baking soda in the milk and set aside. Cream the margarine and brown sugar in a bowl until light and fluffy. Add the eggs and mix well. Add the baking soda mixture and mix well.

Sift the flour, cloves, nutmeg and cinnamon together into a bowl. Add the candied fruits and raisins and toss until coated.

Add the fruit mixture to the margarine mixture and mix well. Add the bourbon gradually, mixing well. Fold in the pecan halves. Drop by teaspoonfuls onto a greased cookie sheet. Bake for 20 minutes. Cool on the cookie sheet for 1 minute and remove to wire racks to cool completely.

Yield: 10 dozen

Energy Saver: To keep humidity as low as possible in your home during hot weather, use covered pans and as little water as necessary for cooking.

Forgotten Cookies

2 egg whites
2/3 cup sugar
1/8 teaspoon salt

1 teaspoon vanilla extract
1 cup chopped nuts
1 cup semisweet chocolate chips

Preheat the gas oven to 350 degrees. Cover cookie sheets with foil. Beat the egg whites in a mixing bowl until soft peaks form. Add the sugar gradually, beating until stiff peaks form. Fold in the salt, vanilla extract, nuts and chocolate chips. Drop by teaspoonfuls on the prepared cookie sheets. Place the cookie sheets in the preheated oven. Turn off the oven. Let the cookie sheets stand in the closed oven overnight. Remove the cookies from the cookie sheets carefully and store in an airtight container.

Yield: 2 dozen

Cookie Jar Gingersnaps

2 cups sifted flour
2 teaspoons baking soda
1/2 teaspoon salt
1 teaspoon cinnamon
1 teaspoon ginger
1 teaspoon ground cloves

3/4 cup shortening
1 cup sugar
1 egg
1/4 cup molasses
Sugar

Preheat the gas oven to 350 degrees. Sift the flour, baking soda, salt, cinnamon, ginger and cloves together and set aside. Cream the shortening and sugar in a bowl until light and fluffy. Add the egg and molasses and beat until smooth. Stir in the sifted flour mixture.

Shape the dough by teaspoonfuls into balls. Roll each ball in sugar and place 2 inches apart on an ungreased cookie sheet. Bake for 10 to 12 minutes. Cool on the cookie sheet for 1 minute and remove to wire racks to cool completely.

Unbaked cookies may be arranged one layer deep in a shallow pan, frozen, removed to plastic bags and stored in the freezer. Remove frozen cookies, arrange on cookie sheets and bake at 350 degrees for 12 to 15 minutes.

Yield: 4 to 5 dozen

Greek Butter Cookies

2 cups (4 sticks) unsalted butter, softened
1/2 cup confectioners' sugar
2 egg yolks
6 cups sifted flour
1 teaspoon baking powder

1 cup almonds, toasted and chopped
2 tablespoons whiskey
1 to 2 (1-pound) packages confectioners' sugar

Preheat the gas oven to 350 degrees. Beat the butter in a bowl for 15 to 20 minutes. Add 1/2 cup confectioners' sugar and beat until light and fluffy. Add the egg yolks and beat thoroughly. Sift the flour and baking powder into a large bowl and stir in the butter mixture. Add the almonds and mix well. Sprinkle the dough with the whiskey, tossing with a fork to mix.

Knead on a lightly floured surface until the dough is firm but pliable. Roll 1/4 to 1/2 inch thick and cut with a cookie cutter. Arrange on a nonstick or lightly greased cookie sheet. Bake for 20 minutes or until lightly brown.

Cool slightly and roll in confectioners' sugar to coat completely. Store in a covered container.

Yield: 5 dozen

Macaroons

1 (14-ounce) package coconut
2/3 cup sugar
6 tablespoons flour
1/4 teaspoon salt

4 egg whites
1 teaspoon almond extract
1 teaspoon vanilla extract

Preheat the gas oven to 350 degrees. Combine the coconut, sugar, flour and salt in a large bowl and mix well. Add the egg whites, almond extract and vanilla extract and mix well. Drop by teaspoonfuls onto a lightly greased and floured cookie sheet. Bake for 20 minutes or until the edges of the cookies are golden brown. Remove immediately and cool on a wire rack. May substitute matzo meal for flour for Passover.

Yield: 2 to 3 dozen

Pecan Tassies

1/2 cup (1 stick) margarine, softened
3 ounces cream cheese, softened
1 cup flour

1/2 cup finely chopped pecans
Pecan Filling (below)

Combine the margarine and cream cheese in a bowl and beat until smooth and creamy. Add the flour 1/4 cup at a time, mixing well after each addition. Knead on a lightly floured surface until smooth. Chill the pastry, covered, for 1 hour.

Preheat the gas oven to 350 degrees. Shape into 1 1/4-inch balls. Press over the bottoms and sides of greased miniature muffin cups. Sprinkle half the pecans into the pastry shells. Fill the shells 2/3 full with the Pecan Filling and sprinkle with the remaining pecans. Bake for 15 to 17 minutes or until filling is almost set.

Reduce the oven temperature to 250 degrees. Bake for 10 minutes longer. Cool completely. Remove from the muffin cups carefully.

Yield: 2 dozen

Pecan Filling

1 egg, slightly beaten
3/4 cup packed brown sugar
1 tablespoon margarine, melted

Dash of salt
2 drops vanilla extract

Place the egg in a bowl and add the brown sugar gradually, beating constantly. Add the margarine, salt and vanilla extract and mix well.

Energy Saver: Keep a log of energy consumption from the information supplied on your regular bills. Add notes for each time period such as weather extremes or house guests. Unexplained variations in usage may need investigating.

Easy Sugar Cookies

1 cup (2 sticks) margarine, softened
1 cup sugar
1 cup confectioners' sugar
2 eggs
3/4 cup vegetable oil
1 teaspoon vanilla extract
1/2 teaspoon baking soda

1/2 teaspoon cream of tartar
5 1/4 cups flour
Granulated sugar
Decorations such as colored sugar, raisins,
  small candies, cherries or chocolate drops
  (optional)

Preheat the gas oven to 350 degrees. Cream the margarine, sugar and confectioners' sugar in a bowl until light and fluffy. Add the eggs 1 at a time, beating well after each addition. Add the oil and vanilla extract and mix well. Combine the baking soda, cream of tartar and flour and add to the creamed mixture gradually, mixing well. Shape into 1-inch balls and arrange on an ungreased cookie sheet. Flatten each ball with a glass dipped in sugar. Sprinkle with additional sugar if desired or decorate as desired. Bake 10 to 12 minutes or until lightly golden. Cool on cookie sheet for 1 minute and remove to wire racks to cool completely.

Yield: 7 dozen

Filled Sugar Cookies

1 recipe Easy Sugar Cookies   Fruit Filling (below)

Chill the Easy Sugar Cookie dough until firm enough to roll. Preheat the gas oven to 350 degrees. Roll the dough on a lightly floured surface, cut with a cookie cutter and arrange half the cookies on an ungreased cookie sheet. Place a teaspoon of the Fruit Filling on each cookie, top with the remaining cookies and press the edges together to seal and enclose the filling. Bake and cool as for Easy Sugar Cookies.

Yield: 3 1/2 to 4 dozen

Fruit Filling

1 cup ground raisins
1/2 cup packed brown sugar

1/2 cup water
1/2 cup chopped nuts

Combine the raisins, brown sugar and water in a saucepan and cook over a low flame until thick, stirring frequently. Stir in the chopped nuts. Cool completely.

Raspberry Almond Shortbread Thumbprints

1 cup (2 sticks) margarine or butter, softened
2/3 cup sugar
1/2 teaspoon almond extract
2 cups flour

2/3 cup raspberry jam
1 cup confectioners' sugar
1 1/2 teaspoons almond extract
2 to 3 teaspoons water

Preheat the gas oven to 350 degrees. Cream the margarine and sugar in a bowl until light and fluffy. Add 1/2 teaspoon almond extract and mix well. Add the flour gradually, mixing well. Chill, covered, for 1 hour.

Shape the dough into 1-inch balls and place 2 inches apart on greased cookie sheets. Make an indentation in each cookie with thumb. Fill each indentation with 1/2 teaspoon jam. Bake for 14 to 18 minutes or until edges are lightly browned. Cool on the cookie sheet for 1 minute and remove to wire racks to cool completely.

Combine the confectioners' sugar, 1 1/2 teaspoons almond extract and water in a small bowl and mix until smooth. Drizzle over the cooled cookies.

Yield: 1 1/2 dozen

Mexican Wedding Cakes

1 cup (2 sticks) margarine, softened
1/2 cup confectioners' sugar
1 teaspoon vanilla extract

2 1/4 cups flour
1/4 teaspoon salt
3/4 cup finely chopped nuts

Preheat the gas oven to 400 degrees. Cream the margarine, sugar and vanilla extract in a large bowl. Combine the flour and salt and add to the creamed mixture gradually. Fold in the nuts. Shape the dough into 1-inch balls and place on an ungreased baking sheet. Bake for 10 to 12 minutes or until firm but not brown.

Roll the warm cookies in confectioners' sugar and place on wire racks to cool. Roll in confectioners' sugar again. Store in airtight containers.

Yield: 3 dozen

Oklahoma Millionaires

1 cup sugar
1 cup packed brown sugar
1 cup light corn syrup
1 cup (2 sticks) margarine, softened
1 (12-ounce) can evaporated milk

1 teaspoon vanilla extract
4 cups pecans
2 cups semisweet chocolate chips
2 cups milk chocolate chips
2 tablespoons paraffin

Combine the sugar, brown sugar, corn syrup, margarine and 1 cup of the evaporated milk in a saucepan over a medium flame and bring to a boil, stirring constantly. Add the remaining evaporated milk gradually, stirring constantly. Cook to 234 to 240 degrees on a candy thermometer, soft-ball stage. Add the vanilla extract and pecans and mix well. Pour into a greased 9×9-inch dish.

Chill, covered, for several hours. Cut into squares. Combine the chocolate chips and paraffin in the top of a double boiler and melt, stirring constantly. Dip the squares into the melted chocolate and place on waxed paper. Let stand until firm.

Yield: 5 to 6 dozen

Toffee Butter Crunch

1 cup (2 sticks) butter or margarine
1¹/₃ cups sugar
1 tablespoon light corn syrup
3 tablespoons water

³/₄ cup coarsely chopped almonds, toasted
2 (7-ounce) milk chocolate bars
1 cup finely chopped almonds, toasted

Melt the butter in a large saucepan over a medium-high flame. Add the sugar, corn syrup and water and mix well. Cook to 295 to 300 degrees on a candy thermometer, hard-crack stage, stirring occasionally. Stir in the coarsely chopped almonds and spread into a greased 9×13-inch pan. Cool completely.

Invert the cooled toffee onto waxed paper. Melt the chocolate, spread half over the toffee and sprinkle with half the finely chopped almonds. Cover with waxed paper, invert, spread with the remaining chocolate and sprinkle with the remaining almonds. Let stand to cool until firm. Break into pieces.

Yield: 2¹/₂ pounds

Dutch Oven Candy

2 cups (4 sticks) butter, melted
1 (12-ounce) can evaporated milk
3/4 cup dark corn syrup

7 cups sugar
3 cups chopped nuts
1 teaspoon vanilla extract

Preheat the gas oven to 275 degrees. Combine the butter, evaporated milk, corn syrup and sugar in a large Dutch oven or other ovenproof container. Bake for 3 1/4 hours or to 240 to 248 degrees on a candy thermometer, firm-ball stage, stirring occasionally. Let stand to cool for 1 hour.

Beat with an electric mixer for 10 minutes. Add the nuts and vanilla extract and mix well. Pour into a large buttered jelly roll pan. Let stand to cool until set. Cut into 1-inch squares.

Yield: 5 pounds

Divinity

2 1/2 cups sugar
1/2 cup light corn syrup
1/2 cup water
1/4 teaspoon salt

2 egg whites
1 teaspoon vanilla extract
1 cup chopped nuts

Combine the sugar, corn syrup, water and salt in a saucepan over a medium flame and bring to a boil, stirring constantly. Reduce the flame and cook to 248 degrees on a candy thermometer, firm-ball stage; do not stir.

Beat the egg whites in a mixing bowl until stiff but not dry peaks form. Add about half the hot syrup gradually, beating constantly. Cook the remaining syrup to 272 degrees. Add the hot syrup to the beaten mixture gradually, beating constantly. Beat at high speed until the mixture is thickened and loses its gloss.

Stir in the vanilla extract and nuts. Drop by teaspoonfuls onto waxed paper. Let stand until cool.

Yield: 1 1/4 pounds

Buttermilk Pralines

2¹/₂ cups sugar
1 teaspoon baking soda
1 cup buttermilk

¹/₄ teaspoon salt
3 tablespoons margarine, softened
3 cups pecan halves

Combine the sugar, baking soda, buttermilk and salt in an 8-quart saucepan. Cook over a medium flame for 5 minutes or to 210 degrees on a candy thermometer, stirring frequently. Add the margarine and 2¹/₃ cups of the pecans. Cook to 230 degrees, spun-thread stage. Let stand to cool for 1 to 2 minutes.

Beat until thick and creamy. Drop by tablespoonfuls onto buttered foil. Top each with a pecan half.

Yield: 4 dozen

Old-Fashioned Peanut Brittle

2 cups sugar
1 cup light corn syrup
¹/₂ cup water

1 cup (2 sticks) margarine
2 cups raw peanuts
1 teaspoon baking soda

Combine the sugar, corn syrup and water in a 3-quart saucepan and bring to a boil over a medium flame, stirring constantly. Add the margarine and mix well. Cook to 230 degrees on a candy thermometer, spun-thread stage. Cook to 280 degrees, stirring frequently. Stir in the peanuts. Cook to 305 degrees, hard-crack stage, stirring constantly.

Remove from the flame and stir in the baking soda quickly. Pour onto 2 buttered foil-lined baking sheets. Cool completely. Break into pieces.

Yield: 2¹/₂ pounds

Peppermint Bark

16 ounces white chocolate
1/2 cup finely crushed peppermint candy
4 to 7 drops red food coloring

Melt the white chocolate in a small saucepan over a low flame, stirring constantly. Stir in the peppermint candy and food coloring. Pour onto a buttered foil-lined baking sheet. Place in the freezer for 5 to 10 minutes or until firm. Peel off the foil and break the candy into pieces.

Yield: 1 1/2 pounds

Old-Fashioned Taffy Apples

2 cups sugar
1/2 cup light corn syrup
3/4 cup water
Red food coloring (optional)
6 apples, washed, dried

Combine the sugar, corn syrup and water in a saucepan and cook over a low flame until the sugar dissolves, stirring constantly. Add the food coloring and mix well. Cook to 300 degrees on a candy thermometer, hard-crack stage.

Pierce a wooden skewer through the stem end of each apple. Place the saucepan of syrup over boiling water to keep hot. Plunge the apples into the hot syrup and turn to coat. Twirl the apples while removing from the syrup and place on buttered foil to cool.

Yield: 6 servings

On October 12, 1981, Oklahoma Natural Gas Company celebrated its 75th year of service to the citizens of Oklahoma. The 75th anniversary celebration spanned a year. Open houses were held and time capsules were buried. Also, an energy conservation display toured the state, appearing at shopping centers and office buildings.

Julie Benell was anchorwoman and Millie Clark was a program guest on a broadcast of "Women Commandoes," a daily show in the early 1940s the Home Service Department aired to provide helpful solutions to wartime family living needs.

Desserts

Norwegian Apple Pie Cake

1 cup sugar
1 cup (2 sticks) margarine
1 egg
1 cup flour
1/4 teaspoon salt
1 teaspoon baking soda

1 teaspoon nutmeg
1 teaspoon cinnamon
2 tablespoons hot water
2 1/2 cups diced peeled apples
1/2 cup chopped nuts
Rum Sauce (below)

Preheat the gas oven to 325 degrees. Cream the sugar and margarine in a mixing bowl until light and fluffy. Beat in the egg. Mix the flour, salt, baking soda, nutmeg and cinnamon together. Mix the flour mixture into the creamed mixture. Add the hot water and mix well.

Fold in the apples and nuts. Pour into a greased and floured 9-inch pie pan. Bake for 40 minutes or until the cake tests done. Serve warm with the Rum Sauce. The cake may be frozen and rewarmed.

Yield: 6 to 8 servings

Rum Sauce

1/2 cup packed brown sugar
1/2 cup heavy cream

1/4 cup rum or apple juice

Combine the brown sugar and cream in a saucepan and cook over a medium flame until the sugar dissolves, stirring constantly. Bring the mixture to a boil and cook for 1 minute, stirring frequently. Remove from the flame, add the rum and mix well.

Yield: 3/4 cup

Energy Saver: *Before the beginning of each heating season, have a technician check your gas-fired furnace to make certain it is working properly and to clean and adjust the burner if necessary.*

Apricot Gold Cake

1 cup (2 sticks) margarine, softened
1 cup sugar
5 eggs
1/2 cup apricot jam
1/2 cup sour cream
1 teaspoon vanilla extract
2 cups flour
1 teaspoon baking soda
1/2 teaspoon salt
2 cups shredded coconut
1 cup finely chopped pecans
1 (8-ounce) package dried apricots, finely chopped
Apricot Glaze (below)

Preheat the gas oven to 350 degrees. Cream the margarine and sugar in a mixing bowl until light and fluffy. Add the eggs 1 at a time, mixing well after each addition. Stir in the jam, sour cream and vanilla extract. Sift the flour, baking soda and salt together. Combine the coconut, pecans and apricots in a bowl.

Add a small amount of the flour mixture and toss until well mixed. Add the remaining flour mixture to the jam mixture and mix well. Fold in the coconut, pecans and apricots. Pour into a greased and floured 10-inch tube pan. Bake for 45 to 55 minutes or until the cake tests done. Cool in the pan for 10 minutes and remove to a wire rack to cool completely. Drizzle the Apricot Glaze over the cooled cake. Store the cake in an airtight container.

Yield: 20 servings

Apricot Glaze

1/2 cup apricot jam
2 tablespoons apricot nectar

Combine the jam and nectar in a small saucepan over a medium flame and cook until well blended, stirring constantly.

Caramel-Filled Chocolate Cake

1 (14-ounce) package caramels, unwrapped
1/2 cup (1 stick) margarine, softened
1 (14-ounce) can sweetened condensed milk

1 (2-layer) package chocolate fudge cake mix
1 1/4 cups chopped pecans

Preheat the gas oven to 350 degrees. Melt the caramels and margarine in a saucepan over a low flame, stirring constantly. Remove from the flame and stir in the condensed milk until smooth.

Prepare the cake mix according to the package directions. Pour 2 cups of the cake batter into a greased 9×13-inch cake pan. Bake for 15 minutes or until the cake tests done. Pour the caramel mixture evenly over the cake. Spoon the remaining batter on top to cover the caramel layer and sprinkle with pecans. Bake for 30 to 35 minutes or until cake tests done. Cool in the pan before cutting.

Yield: 15 servings

Earthquake Cake

1 cup coconut
1 cup coarsely chopped pecans
1 (2-layer) package German chocolate
   cake mix

1/2 cup (1 stick) margarine, softened
8 ounces cream cheese, softened
1 (1-pound) package confectioners' sugar
1 teaspoon vanilla extract

Preheat the gas oven to 350 degrees. Grease and flour a 9×13-inch cake pan. Sprinkle the coconut and pecans evenly over the bottom and set aside. Prepare the cake mix according to the package instructions and pour into the prepared pan.

Cream the margarine, cream cheese and confectioners' sugar in a mixing bowl until light and fluffy. Add the vanilla extract and mix well. Spoon the cream cheese mixture randomly over the cake batter. Bake for 45 to 50 minutes or until the cake tests done. Cool in the pan. The cake will rise while baking then fall as it cools.

Yield: 15 servings

German's Sweet Chocolate Cake

1 (4-ounce) package German's sweet
   chocolate
1/2 cup boiling water
1 teaspoon vanilla extract
1 cup (2 sticks) margarine, softened
2 cups sugar
4 egg yolks

2 1/2 cups sifted cake flour
1 teaspoon baking soda
1/2 teaspoon salt
1 cup buttermilk
4 egg whites, stiffly beaten
Coconut Frosting (below)

Preheat the gas oven to 350 degrees. Melt the chocolate in the boiling water, stirring to blend well. Add the vanilla extract and set aside. Cream the margarine and sugar in a mixing bowl until light and fluffy. Add the egg yolks 1 at a time, mixing well after each addition. Sift the flour, baking soda and salt together and add to the creamed mixture alternately with the buttermilk, mixing well after each addition. Add the melted chocolate and mix well.

Fold in the egg whites gently. Pour into 2 greased and floured 10-inch layer cake pans or three 8-inch layer cake pans. Bake for 30 to 35 minutes or until cake tests done. Cool the layers in the pans for 10 minutes and remove to wire racks to cool completely. Spread the Coconut Frosting between the layers and over the top and side of the cooled cake.

Yield: 15 servings

Coconut Frosting

1 cup evaporated milk
1 cup sugar
3 egg yolks
1/2 cup (1 stick) margarine, softened

1 teaspoon vanilla extract
1 cup pecans
1 (3-ounce) can flaked coconut

Combine the evaporated milk, sugar, egg yolks, margarine and vanilla extract in a saucepan and cook over a medium flame until thickened, stirring constantly. Add the pecans and coconut and mix well.

Brownie Sheet Cake

1 cup water
1 cup (2 sticks) margarine
1/4 cup baking cocoa
2 cups flour
2 cups sugar

1 teaspoon baking soda
1 to 2 teaspoons cinnamon
2 eggs
1/2 cup buttermilk
Chocolate Pecan Frosting (below)

Preheat the gas oven to 400 degrees. Combine the water, margarine and baking cocoa in a large saucepan and bring to a boil over a medium flame, stirring frequently. Remove from the flame.

Sift the flour, sugar, baking soda and cinnamon together, add to the chocolate mixture and blend well. Beat in the eggs and buttermilk. Pour into a greased and floured large jelly roll pan. Bake for 20 minutes or until the cake tests done.

Frost the warm cake with Chocolate Pecan Frosting. Cool completely.

Yield: 15 servings

Chocolate Pecan Frosting

1/3 cup buttermilk
1/2 cup (1 stick) margarine
1/4 cup baking cocoa

1 (1-pound) package confectioners' sugar,
   sifted
1 cup chopped pecans

Combine the buttermilk and margarine in a saucepan and bring to a boil over a medium flame. Sift the cocoa and confectioners' sugar together into a mixing bowl. Add the buttermilk mixture and beat until creamy. Stir in the pecans.

Energy Saver: *During winter months, open draperies, shades, or blinds on sunny days to utilize the heat from the sun; close them at night.*

Best Ever Chocolate Cake

1/2 cup shortening
1 1/2 cups sugar
1 egg, beaten
1/4 cup baking cocoa
1 teaspoon red food coloring (optional)
2 tablespoons hot strong coffee

2 cups sifted cake flour
1 teaspoon salt
1 teaspoon baking soda
1 cup buttermilk
1 teaspoon vanilla extract
Fudge Nut Frosting (below)

Preheat the gas oven to 375 degrees. Cream the shortening and sugar in a mixing bowl until light and fluffy. Add the egg and mix well. Combine the baking cocoa, food coloring and hot coffee in a small bowl and mix to form a smooth paste. Add to the creamed mixture and mix well.

Sift the flour, salt and baking soda together. Add to the creamed mixture alternately with the buttermilk, mixing well after each addition. Add the vanilla extract and mix well. Pour into 2 greased and floured 8×8-inch cake pans. Bake for 30 to 35 minutes or until cake tests done. Cool in the pans for 10 minutes and remove to wire racks to cool completely. Spread the Fudge Nut Frosting between the layers and over the top and sides of the cooled cake.

Yield: 8 servings

Fudge Nut Frosting

1 ounce chocolate, finely chopped
1 cup sugar
1/3 cup milk
1/4 cup (1/2 stick) butter

1/4 teaspoon salt
1 teaspoon vanilla extract
1/4 cup chopped nuts

Combine the chocolate, sugar, milk, butter and salt in a saucepan and bring to a boil over a medium flame, stirring constantly. Boil for 1 minute. Add the vanilla extract.

Beat until the mixture is of spreading consistency. Fold in the nuts.

German's Chocolate Oat Cake

1¼ cups boiling water
1 cup quick-cooking oats
½ cup (1 stick) margarine
1 (4-ounce) package German's sweet
   chocolate, broken
1½ cups sifted flour

1 cup sugar
1 teaspoon baking soda
½ teaspoon salt
1 cup packed brown sugar
3 eggs, beaten
Caramel Nut Topping (below)

Preheat the gas oven to 350 degrees. Combine the boiling water, oats, margarine and chocolate in a mixing bowl. Let stand for 20 minutes and mix well. Sift the flour, sugar, baking soda and salt together into a large bowl. Add the brown sugar, eggs and oats mixture and beat at low speed just until thoroughly combined. Pour into a greased and floured 9×13-inch cake pan. Bake for 35 to 40 minutes or until the cake tests done.

Preheat the gas broiler. Spread Caramel Nut Topping evenly over the hot cake. Broil 4 to 5 inches from the flame for 1 minute or until bubbly. Serve warm or cool.

Yield: 15 servings

Caramel Nut Topping

6 tablespoons margarine, softened
¼ cup light cream

¾ cup packed brown sugar
½ cup chopped pecans

Combine the margarine, cream and brown sugar in a saucepan and bring to a boil over a medium flame, stirring constantly.

Reduce the flame and simmer for 2 to 3 minutes or until slightly thickened, stirring frequently. Stir in the pecans.

Energy Saver: Fill the dryer before using, but don't overload it. This causes wrinkles requiring ironing.

Italian Cream Cake

1 cup buttermilk
1 teaspoon baking soda
5 egg whites
1/2 cup (1 stick) margarine, softened
1/2 cup shortening
2 cups sugar

5 egg yolks
2 cups sifted flour
1 teaspoon vanilla extract
1 cup chopped pecans
1 (3-ounce) can coconut
Cream Cheese Icing (below)

Preheat the gas oven to 350 degrees. Combine the buttermilk and baking soda in a small bowl, mix well and set aside. Beat the egg whites until stiff peaks form and set aside.

Cream the margarine, shortening and sugar in a mixing bowl until light and fluffy. Add the egg yolks 1 at a time, beating well after each addition. Add the flour alternately with the buttermilk mixture, mixing well after each addition. Add the vanilla extract and blend well. Fold in the egg whites gently.

Fold in the pecans and coconut gently. Pour into 3 greased and floured 9-inch layer cake pans. Bake for 25 to 30 minutes or until cake tests done. Cool in the pan for 10 minutes and remove to wire racks to cool completely.

Spread Cream Cheese Icing between the layers and over the top and side of the cake.

Yield: 12 servings

Cream Cheese Icing

8 ounces cream cheese, softened
1/2 cup (1 stick) margarine, softened

1 teaspoon vanilla extract
1 (1-pound) package confectioners' sugar

Beat the cream cheese and margarine in a bowl until light and fluffy. Add the vanilla extract and blend well. Beat in enough of the confectioners' sugar gradually to make the frosting of the desired spreading consistency.

Macaroon Cupcakes

1 cup sugar
3/4 cup flour
1/2 teaspoon baking powder
1/2 teaspoon salt
6 egg whites
1/2 teaspoon cream of tartar

1/3 cup sugar
1/2 teaspoon vanilla extract
1/2 teaspoon almond extract
1 (3-ounce) can sweetened flaked coconut
Sliced almonds

Preheat the gas oven to 300 degrees. Combine 1 cup sugar, flour, baking powder and salt and set aside. Beat the egg whites and cream of tartar at low speed in a mixing bowl until foamy. Add 1/3 cup sugar gradually, beating constantly at high speed until stiff peaks form. Beat in the vanilla and almond extracts.

Fold the flour mixture and coconut into the egg white mixture gently. Fill 24 paper-lined muffin cups 2/3 full. Top with sliced almonds. Bake for 30 minutes or just until cupcakes begin to brown. Cool in the muffin cups for 10 minutes and remove to wire racks.

Yield: 24 cupcakes

Glorious Pound Cake

2 cups (4 sticks) butter
1 (1-pound) package confectioners' sugar
6 eggs

1 1/2 teaspoons vanilla extract
3 cups sifted cake flour

Preheat the gas oven to 325 degrees. Cream the butter and confectioners' sugar in a mixing bowl until light and fluffy. Add the eggs 1 at a time, beating well after each addition. Add the vanilla extract and blend well. Stir in the flour gradually. Pour into a greased and floured 10-inch tube pan. Bake for 1 hour and 10 minutes or until the cake tests done. Cool in the pan for 10 minutes and invert onto a wire rack to cool completely.

Yield: 16 servings

Pumpkin Cake Roll

3 eggs
1 cup sugar
2/3 cup canned pumpkin
1 teaspoon lemon juice
3/4 cup flour
1 teaspoon baking powder
2 teaspoons cinnamon

1 teaspoon ginger
1/2 teaspoon nutmeg
1/2 teaspoon salt
1 cup finely chopped walnuts
Confectioners' sugar
Cream Cheese Filling (below)

Preheat the gas oven to 375 degrees. Beat the eggs in a mixing bowl at high speed for 5 minutes. Add the sugar gradually, beating constantly. Stir in the pumpkin and lemon juice. Combine the flour, baking powder, cinnamon, ginger, nutmeg and salt and fold into the pumpkin mixture. Spread in a greased and floured 10×15-inch jelly roll pan. Sprinkle with walnuts. Bake for 15 minutes or until the cake tests done.

Dust a clean kitchen towel generously with confectioners' sugar. Invert the cake onto the towel. Roll the warm cake in the towel as for a jelly roll from the short side and place on a wire rack to cool.

Unroll the cooled cake carefully and remove the towel. Trim the cake edges if necessary. Spread the Cream Cheese Filling within 1 inch of the edges of the cake and reroll. Wrap in plastic wrap and chill in the refrigerator.

Yield: 8 servings

Cream Cheese Filling

6 ounces cream cheese, softened
1/4 cup (1/2 stick) margarine, softened

1 cup confectioners' sugar
1/2 teaspoon vanilla extract

Cream the cream cheese, margarine and confectioners' sugar in a bowl until light and fluffy. Add the vanilla extract and blend well.

Strawberry Cake

1 (2-layer) package white cake mix
3 tablespoons flour, sifted
1 (3-ounce) package strawberry gelatin
1/2 cup water

3/4 cup vegetable oil
4 eggs
1/2 cup frozen strawberries, thawed
Strawberry Frosting (below)

Preheat the gas oven to 350 degrees. Combine the cake mix, flour, gelatin, water, oil and eggs in a mixing bowl and beat for 2 minutes or until smooth. Add the strawberries and beat for 1 minute or until thoroughly mixed. Pour into 2 greased and floured 9-inch layer cake pans. Bake for 30 to 35 minutes or until cake tests done. Cool in the pan for 10 minutes and remove to wire racks to cool completely.

Spread Strawberry Frosting between the layers and over the top and side of the cake. May substitute raspberry gelatin and frozen raspberries to make raspberry cake.

Yield: 12 servings

Strawberry Frosting

1/2 cup (1 stick) margarine, softened
1 (1-pound) package confectioners' sugar

1/4 teaspoon salt
1/2 cup (about) frozen strawberries, thawed

Cream the margarine and confectioners' sugar in a bowl until light and fluffy. Add the salt and blend well. Add enough strawberries to make the frosting of spreading consistency, beating constantly.

Energy Saver: Do not overdry fabrics. Some moisture left in the fabric helps prevent wrinkling and ironing is less necessary.

Farmers' Apple Pie

1 unbaked (9-inch) pie shell
3 cups shredded peeled apples (Delicious, Winesap or Macintosh)
3/4 cup sugar

1/2 teaspoon cinnamon
1/4 teaspoon nutmeg
Dash of salt
1 cup heavy cream

Preheat the gas oven to 450 degrees. Bake the pie shell for 8 minutes. Reduce the oven temperature to 350 degrees. Combine the apples, sugar, cinnamon, nutmeg, salt and cream in a bowl and mix well. Pour the apple mixture into the baked pie shell. Bake for 1 hour.

Yield: 6 servings

Blueberry Sour Cream Pie

2 cups sour cream
3 tablespoons flour
3 tablespoons light brown sugar
1 egg, beaten

1 (9-inch) graham cracker pie shell
2 cups blueberries, rinsed, drained
1/2 cup packed light brown sugar

Preheat the gas oven to 400 degrees. Combine the sour cream, flour and 3 tablespoons brown sugar in a bowl and mix well. Beat in the egg. Spoon half the mixture into the pie shell.

Combine the blueberries and 1/2 cup brown sugar in a bowl and mix gently. Pour into the pie shell and top with the remaining sour cream mixture. Bake for 10 to 15 minutes or until set. Let stand until cool. Chill until ready to serve. Serve with a dollop of additional sour cream and garnish with additional blueberries.

Yield: 6 to 8 servings

Buttermilk Pie

1/2 cup (1 stick) butter, softened
1 1/2 cups sugar
3 tablespoons flour
3 eggs, beaten

1 cup buttermilk
1 teaspoon vanilla extract
Dash of nutmeg
1 unbaked (9-inch) pie shell

Preheat the gas oven to 350 degrees. Cream the butter and sugar in a bowl until light and fluffy. Beat in the flour gradually. Add the eggs and beat well. Add the buttermilk, vanilla extract and nutmeg and blend well. Pour into the pie shell. Bake for 45 to 50 minutes or until set. Let stand until cool. Serve with whipped cream.

Yield: 6 to 8 servings

Cherry Delight Pie

8 ounces graham crackers, crushed
1/2 cup (1 stick) margarine, softened
8 ounces cream cheese, softened

1 cup confectioners' sugar
1 cup whipping cream
1 (22-ounce) can cherry pie filling, chilled

Combine the graham crackers and margarine in a bowl and mix well. Press the crumb mixture over the bottom and up the side of a 10-inch pie pan. Chill until firm.

Combine the cream cheese, confectioners' sugar and whipping cream in a bowl and beat until fluffy. Spoon the cream cheese mixture into the pie shell and chill for 2 hours or longer. Top with the cherry pie filling just before serving.

Yield: 6 servings

Energy Saver: *Turn off the pilot light on your gas furnace in the summer.*

German's Chocolate Pie

1 (4-ounce) package German's sweet
   chocolate
1/4 cup (1/2 stick) margarine
1 2/3 cup evaporated milk
1 1/2 cups sugar
3 tablespoons cornstarch

1/8 teaspoon salt
2 eggs
1 teaspoon vanilla extract
1 unbaked (9-inch) pie shell
1 1/3 cups coconut
1/2 cup chopped pecans

Preheat the gas oven to 375 degrees. Melt the chocolate and margarine in a saucepan over a low flame, stirring constantly. Remove from the flame, blend in the evaporated milk and set aside.

Combine the sugar, cornstarch and salt in a bowl and mix well. Beat in the eggs and vanilla extract. Add the chocolate mixture and blend well. Pour into the pie shell and sprinkle with coconut and pecans. Bake for 10 minutes.

Cover loosely with foil. Bake for 40 minutes longer or until the center is soft and the top puffs and cracks. Let stand to cool for 4 hours or longer before serving.

Yield: 8 to 10 servings

Kentucky Pie

1 cup sugar
1/2 cup flour
1/2 cup (1 stick) margarine, melted
2 eggs, slightly beaten

1 teaspoon vanilla extract
1 cup chocolate chips
1 cup nuts
1 unbaked (9-inch) pie shell

Preheat the gas oven to 325 degrees. Combine the sugar, flour and margarine in a bowl and mix well. Stir in the eggs and vanilla. Add the chocolate chips and nuts and mix well. Pour into the pie shell. Bake for 1 hour or until golden brown. Let stand until completely cooled.

Yield: 6 servings

Coconut Pie

2/3 cup graham cracker crumbs
1/3 cup soda cracker crumbs
1 2/3 teaspoons baking powder
2/3 cup shredded coconut

1/3 cup chopped pecans
2/3 cup egg whites
1 1/3 cups sugar
1 teaspoon vanilla extract

Preheat the gas oven to 350 degrees. Combine the graham and soda cracker crumbs, baking powder, coconut and pecans in a bowl and mix well. Beat the egg whites and 2/3 cup of the sugar in a mixing bowl until stiff peaks form. Beat in the remaining 2/3 cup sugar gradually until the sugar is dissolved. Add the vanilla extract and blend well. Fold the dry ingredients into the egg whites gently. Spread into a lightly greased and floured 8- or 9-inch pie plate. Bake for 25 to 30 minutes or until golden. Let stand until cooled completely. Serve with whipped cream.

Yield: 6 to 8 servings

Eggnog Pie

1 teaspoon unflavored gelatin
1 tablespoon cold water
1 cup milk
1/2 cup sugar
2 tablespoons cornstarch
1/4 teaspoon salt

3 egg yolks, beaten
1 tablespoon margarine
1 teaspoon vanilla extract
1 cup whipping cream, whipped
1 baked (9-inch) pie shell
Nutmeg to taste

Sprinkle the gelatin over the cold water and set aside to soften. Scald the milk in a large saucepan over a low flame. Combine the sugar, cornstarch and salt, mix well and add to the scalded milk. Cook until thickened and smooth, stirring constantly. Cook for 15 minutes longer, stirring constantly. Stir a small amount of the hot milk mixture into the egg yolks; stir the egg yolks into the milk mixture. Cook for several minutes, stirring frequently.

Place the egg mixture over hot water or pour into the top of a double boiler over hot water. Add the softened gelatin and margarine and stir until the gelatin dissolves and the margarine melts. Remove from the flame and let stand until cooled completely. Add the vanilla extract and mix well. Fold the whipped cream into the custard and pour into the pie shell. Sprinkle generously with nutmeg. Chill until set and ready to serve.

Yield: 6 to 8 servings

Lemon Chess Pie

2 cups sugar
1 tablespoon flour
1 tablespoon cornmeal
4 eggs
1/4 cup (1/2 stick) butter, melted

1/4 cup light cream or milk
2 tablespoons grated lemon zest
1/4 cup lemon juice
1 unbaked (9-inch) pie shell

Preheat the gas oven to 350 degrees. Combine the sugar, flour and cornmeal in a large bowl. Add the eggs, butter, cream and lemon zest and beat for 5 minutes or until well blended. Add the lemon juice and mix well. Pour into the pie shell. Bake for 35 to 40 minutes or until golden brown. Let stand until cool and store the pie in the refrigerator.

Yield: 6 to 8 servings

Key Lime Pie

5 egg yolks
1 (14-ounce) can sweetened condensed milk
3/4 cup fresh key lime juice

3 egg whites
1 baked (9-inch) pie shell, cooled
1 cup whipping cream, whipped (optional)

Preheat the gas oven to 325 degrees. Beat the egg yolks in a large bowl for 3 to 5 minutes or until thick. Beat in the condensed milk gradually. Beat in the lime juice gradually.

Beat the egg whites in a medium bowl until soft peaks form; do not overbeat. Fold the egg whites gently into the lime mixture. Pour into the pie shell. Bake for 20 minutes or until set.

Let stand until cool. Serve at room temperature or chilled. Serve with whipped cream spread over the pie, piped or dolloped decoratively on top or passed separately for individual serving.

Yield: 6 to 8 servings

Crumb Peach Pie

4 cups sliced peeled fresh peaches
1 unbaked (9-inch) pie shell
1/3 cup sugar
Dash of nutmeg
1/2 cup flour

1/4 cup packed brown sugar
1/2 teaspoon cinnamon
1/4 cup (1/2 stick) butter, softened
1/4 cup chopped nuts

Preheat the gas oven to 425 degrees. Arrange the peach slices in the pie shell. Sprinkle with the sugar and nutmeg. Combine the flour, brown sugar and cinnamon in a bowl. Cut in the butter until crumbly. Stir in the nuts and sprinkle the mixture over the peaches.

Bake for 35 to 40 minutes or until golden brown. Let stand until cooled completely before slicing. Garnish with dollops of sour cream.

Yield: 6 to 8 servings

Aunt Carrie's Pecan Pie

1/2 cup (1 stick) butter, melted
3/4 cup sugar
1 cup light corn syrup
4 eggs, beaten

1 teaspoon vanilla extract
1/4 teaspoon salt
1 unbaked (9-inch) pie shell
1 1/2 cups pecan halves

Preheat the gas oven to 325 degrees. Combine the butter, sugar and corn syrup in a saucepan and cook over a low flame until the sugar dissolves, stirring constantly. Add a small amount of the hot mixture to the eggs; add the eggs to the hot mixture and mix well. Add the vanilla and salt and mix well. Pour into the pie shell and sprinkle with pecans. Bake for 50 to 55 minutes or until golden brown. Let stand until cooled completely.

Yield: 6 servings

Favorite Strawberry Pie

3 ounces cream cheese, softened
1 baked (9-inch) pie shell, cooled
1 quart fresh strawberries

1 cup sugar
3 tablespoons cornstarch

Spread the cream cheese over the bottom of the pie shell. Rinse and hull all the strawberries. Select half the whole strawberries, drain well, pat dry and arrange in the prepared pie shell. Mash the remaining strawberries and add enough water to measure 1 1/2 cups. Pour the mashed strawberries into a saucepan and bring to a boil over a medium flame. Mix the sugar and cornstarch together.

Stir the cornstarch mixture into the mashed strawberries gradually, return to the boil and cook for 1 minute, stirring constantly. Let stand until cool. Pour the cooked strawberry mixture over the berries in the pie shell. Chill for 2 hours. Garnish with whipped cream.

Yield: 6 servings

Sour Cream Raisin Pie

1 cup raisins
1 cup hot water
1 cup packed brown sugar
2 tablespoons flour
1/2 teaspoon nutmeg
1/2 teaspoon cinnamon

1/4 teaspoon salt
1 cup sour cream
3 egg yolks, beaten
3 egg whites
6 tablespoons sugar
1 baked (9-inch) pie shell

Plump the raisins in the hot water for several minutes; drain well and set aside. Combine the brown sugar, flour, nutmeg, cinnamon, salt and sour cream in a saucepan and cook over a medium flame until thickened, stirring constantly. Stir a small amount of the sour cream mixture into the egg yolks; stir the egg yolks into the sour cream mixture. Cook for 5 minutes, stirring constantly. Add the raisins and mix well. Remove from the flame. Let stand until cooled completely.

Preheat the gas oven to 350 degrees. Beat the egg whites in a bowl until soft peaks form. Add the sugar gradually, beating until stiff peaks form. Pour the raisin filling into the pie shell. Top with the meringue, sealing to the edge. Bake for 12 minutes or until golden brown.

Yield: 6 to 8 servings

Rhubarb Custard Pie

1 recipe (2-crust) pie pastry
3 cups 1-inch pieces rhubarb
1/2 cup sugar
2 tablespoons cornstarch
1/4 teaspoon salt
1 egg
3/4 cup light corn syrup
1 tablespoon margarine, melted
1 to 2 tablespoons milk (optional)
2 tablespoons (about) sugar (optional)

Preheat the gas oven to 425 degrees. Line a pie plate with half the pastry, leaving 1 1/2 inches beyond outer rim.

Rinse the rhubarb, drain well and place into the pastry-lined pie plate. Combine 1/2 cup sugar, cornstarch and salt in a bowl. Add the egg and beat well. Add the corn syrup and margarine, blend well and pour over the rhubarb.

Roll out the remaining pastry to 1/8-inch thickness and cut into 3/4-inch wide strips. Arrange the pastry strips lattice-fashion over the rhubarb filling. Moisten and secure the pastry strips to the edge, fold the pastry over and flute to make a high rim. Brush the pastry edge with the milk and sprinkle with 2 tablespoons sugar to produce a crisp glaze when baked.

Bake for 15 minutes. Reduce the temperature to 350 degrees. Bake for 30 minutes longer. Let stand until cooled completely.

Yield: 6 servings

Energy Saver: *Keep all heat outlets free of obstructions.*

Swedish Apple Dumplings

6 small tart apples
2 cups flour
4 teaspoons baking powder
1/2 teaspoon salt
1/2 cup shortening
2/3 to 3/4 cup milk
6 tablespoons (about) sugar
Cinnamon Glaze (below)

Preheat the gas oven to 400 degrees. Wash, peel and core the apples and set aside. Sift the flour, baking powder and salt together into a large bowl. Cut in the shortening until crumbly. Add enough milk to form a soft dough, stirring with a fork. Roll the dough thinly on a lightly floured surface. Cut the dough into six 6-inch squares.

Place an apple in the center of each square and spoon about 1 tablespoon sugar into each core. Fold the dough over the apples, pinching the edges to seal completely.

Place the pastry-wrapped apples in a greased baking dish and drizzle with Cinnamon Glaze. Bake for 45 minutes or until the pastry is golden brown. Serve with warm cream.

Yield: 6 servings

Cinnamon Glaze

1 cup water
Dash of cinnamon
1 cup plus 2 tablespoons sugar
1/2 cup (1 stick) margarine

Combine the water, cinnamon, sugar and margarine in a saucepan and bring to a boil over a medium flame, stirring frequently.

In April of 1989, ONG employees constructed an award-winning float that was used in the Land Run Centennial Parades held across the state. The float, depicting the people of the Land Run as well as today's Oklahomans, traveled to more than 40 towns located throughout Oklahoma. Many times, civic leaders requested to ride on the float and greet parade crowds. The float made its final journey January 1, 1999, to Dallas, Texas, to participate in the Cotton Bowl Parade. ONG received numerous cash prizes for its float and donated them to "Share the Warmth," a program to assist customers with heating bills, and to Leadership Oklahoma, Inc., a program designed to develop leadership skills in present and future Oklahoma leaders.

Ben's Bananas Foster

2 tablespoons margarine
4 small bananas, cut lengthwise
2 tablespoons brown sugar

Dash of cinnamon
1 tablespoon banana liqueur
1/2 cup rum

Melt the margarine in a saucepan or skillet over a medium flame. Add the bananas and cook until golden, turning frequently. Sprinkle with the brown sugar and cinnamon.

Remove the bananas to a serving dish and top with the pan juices. Heat the banana liqueur and rum, pour over the bananas and ignite. Serve blazing bananas with ice cream.

Yield: 4 servings

Heavenly Blueberry Dessert

3/4 cup (1 1/2 sticks) margarine
1 1/2 cups flour
2 tablespoons sugar
1 cup finely chopped pecans

11 ounces cream cheese, softened
2 cups confectioners' sugar
8 ounces whipped topping
1 to 2 (21-ounce) cans blueberry pie filling

Preheat the gas oven to 325 degrees. Melt the margarine in a medium saucepan over a low flame. Stir in the flour, sugar and pecans. Press the mixture into a greased 9×13-inch baking dish and bake for 20 minutes. Let stand until cool.

Beat the cream cheese and confectioners' sugar in a bowl until smooth. Stir in the whipped topping. Spread over the cooled crust and top with the blueberry pie filling. Chill overnight.

May substitute a plain unbaked graham cracker crust mixture for the baked pecan crust.

Yield: 12 servings

Cherry Dessert

1 1/2 cups vanilla wafer crumbs
3 tablespoons margarine, melted
1 (14-ounce) can sweetened condensed milk
Juice of 2 lemons
1 (16-ounce) can sour pitted cherries,
    drained

Red food coloring
1 cup pecans
1 cup whipping cream, whipped

Combine the vanilla wafer crumbs and margarine in a bowl and mix well. Press 2/3 of the mixture over the bottom of a 9-inch square baking dish.

Combine the condensed milk and lemon juice in a bowl and mix well. Add the cherries, food coloring and pecans and mix well. Fold in the whipped cream. Pour the mixture into the prepared dish and top with the remaining crumbs.

Chill in the refrigerator or freeze until serving time. Cut into squares. May be served frozen.

Yield: 9 to 12 servings

Frozen Lemon Dessert

3/4 cup vanilla wafer crumbs
3 egg yolks
1/2 cup sugar
1/4 cup lemon juice

2 teaspoons grated lemon zest
3 egg whites
2 tablespoons sugar
1 cup whipping cream, whipped

Sprinkle the vanilla wafer crumbs into a greased 8×8-inch dish and set aside. Place the egg yolks in a saucepan. Add 1/2 cup sugar gradually, beating constantly until light. Cook over a low flame until thickened, stirring constantly. Remove from the flame and let stand until cool. Stir in the lemon juice and zest gradually.

Beat the egg whites in a mixing bowl, adding 2 tablespoons sugar gradually and beating until soft peaks form. Fold the egg whites into the whipped cream. Fold the whipped cream mixture into the cooled custard. Pour into the prepared dish and freeze, covered, for several hours.

Yield: 6 to 8 servings

Strawberry Shortcake

1 quart strawberries, sliced
1 cup sugar
2 cups flour
2 tablespoons sugar
3 teaspoons baking powder

1 teaspoon salt
1/3 cup shortening
1 cup milk
Margarine
Light cream or whipped cream

Sprinkle the strawberries with 1 cup sugar and let stand for 1 hour.

Preheat the gas oven to 425 degrees. Combine the flour, 2 tablespoons sugar, baking powder and salt in a mixing bowl. Cut in the shortening until crumbly. Stir in the milk just until blended. Pat the mixture into a greased 8-inch layer pan. Bake for 15 to 20 minutes or until golden brown. Split the shortcake into 2 layers while warm.

Spread the cut sides with margarine, spoon half the strawberries between the layers and top with the remaining strawberries. Serve warm with cream.

Yield: 8 servings

Easy Strawberry Cobbler

1/4 cup (1/2 stick) margarine
1/2 cup milk
1/2 cup sifted self-rising flour
1/2 cup sugar

2 cups sliced strawberries
1/2 cup sugar
1/2 teaspoon cinnamon

Preheat the gas grill to medium. Melt the margarine in an 8×8-inch baking pan. Combine the milk, flour and 1/2 cup sugar in a bowl and mix well. Pour over the melted margarine; do not stir. Combine the strawberries, 1/2 cup sugar and cinnamon in a bowl, mix well and spoon over the batter; do not stir. Cover the pan with foil.

Place the pan on the grill, close the lid and cook, covered, for 35 minutes or until done.

Yield: 4 servings

Brownie Baked Alaska

1 (15-ounce) package fudge brownie mix
1 pint ice cream
Meringue (below)

Prepare and bake the brownies according to the package directions. Cut the baked layer into 3-inch squares, cool and chill.

Place 9 small scoops of ice cream on a baking sheet lined with parchment paper and freeze for several hours.

Arrange the brownie squares on a parchment paper-lined baking sheet, leaving space between each brownie. Place a scoop of ice cream on top of each brownie square and freeze for 1 hour or longer. Preheat the gas oven to 500 degrees. Spread the brownies and ice cream with the meringue, sealing to the edges. Bake for 3 to 4 minutes or until the meringue is light brown. Serve immediately.

Yield: 9 servings

Meringue

4 egg whites
1/4 teaspoon cream of tartar
1/2 cup sugar

Beat the egg whites and cream of tartar in a mixing bowl until soft peaks form. Add the sugar 1 tablespoon at a time, beating until stiff peaks form.

Energy Saver: When cooking fresh or frozen vegetables, use the smallest possible amount of water, a covered pan, and a low flame.

Company Cheesecake

3 eggs, beaten
16 ounces cream cheese, softened
1 cup sugar
1/4 teaspoon salt

2 teaspoons vanilla extract
1/2 teaspoon almond extract
3 cups sour cream
Graham Nut Crust (below)

Preheat the gas oven to 325 degrees. Combine the eggs, cream cheese, sugar, salt and vanilla and almond extracts in a bowl and beat until smooth. Blend in the sour cream and pour into the Graham Nut Crust. Sprinkle with the reserved graham nut mixture. Bake for 50 to 60 minutes or until set. Let stand until cool. Chill for 4 hours or longer.

Place the cheesecake on a serving plate, loosen the cheesecake from the side of the pan with a sharp knife and remove the side of the pan. Garnish with strawberries.

Yield: 12 to 16 servings

Graham Nut Crust

1 3/4 cups fine graham cracker crumbs
1/2 teaspoon cinnamon

1/4 cup finely chopped walnuts
1/2 cup (1 stick) margarine, melted

Combine the graham cracker crumbs, cinnamon, walnuts and margarine in a bowl and mix well. Reserve 3 tablespoons of the mixture for topping.

Press the remaining mixture over the bottom and 2 1/2 inches up the side of a 9-inch springform pan.

Energy Saver: *Whenever possible cook foods that are compatible by time and temperature in the oven.*

Elegant Champagne Ice

1/4 cup sugar
1 1/2 cups water
3 tablespoons orange liqueur
Rind and juice of 1 lemon
Rind and juice of 2 oranges
3 cups Champagne
2 cups strawberry halves
Sugar to taste

Combine the sugar and water in a saucepan and bring to a boil over a medium flame, stirring occasionally. Cook for 5 minutes, remove from the flame and let stand until cool. Pour the syrup into a freezer container or bowl. Stir the liqueur into the cooled syrup. Cut the lemon and orange rinds into strips. Add several pieces of fruit rind to the syrup and chill for 2 hours.

Remove and discard the rinds. Stir in 2 cups Champagne and the fruit juices. Freeze until the mixture becomes slushy. Beat until smooth and place in the freezer for several hours, stirring occasionally.

Sprinkle the strawberries with a small amount of sugar and the remaining 1 cup Champagne. Chill the strawberries for 4 hours. Place the strawberries in crystal goblets and fill with Champagne Ice.

Yield: 8 servings

Crepes Suzette

3 ounces cream cheese, softened
2 tablespoons maple syrup
10 to 12 crepes (below)
1/3 cup margarine
1/3 cup packed brown sugar

1/3 cup fresh orange juice
Strips of 1 or 2 orange rinds
2 to 3 tablespoons brandy
2 to 3 tablespoons orange liqueur

Combine the cream cheese and maple syrup in a bowl and mix well. Spread the light brown side of each crepe with a thin coating of the cream cheese mixture. Fold in half, and fold in half again to form a triangle. Melt the margarine in a large skillet. Add the brown sugar, orange juice and several strips of orange rind, mix well and bring to a boil over a medium flame. Cook for 1 to 2 minutes. Remove the orange rinds and place the folded crepes in the skillet, forming a ring. Spoon the butter sauce over the crepes. Pour the brandy and liqueur into the center of the skillet and ignite. Remove crepes to dessert plates and top with the sauce.

Yield: 10 to 12 servings

Crepes

3 eggs, beaten
1 teaspoon salt
1 1/2 teaspoons sugar

2 cups milk
3 tablespoons margarine, melted
1 cup less 1 tablespoon flour

Combine the eggs, salt and sugar in a large bowl and beat well. Combine the milk and margarine in a medium bowl and mix well. Add the flour to the egg mixture alternately with the milk mixture, beating well after each addition. Heat a small amount of margarine in a crepe pan over a medium flame. Pour 2 to 3 tablespoons batter into the pan and tilt until the bottom is completely covered. Cook until the underside is light brown and the top is firm. Turn the crepe over and cook for 1 minute longer. Slide the crepe onto waxed paper and cover with waxed paper. Repeat until all batter is used, adding additional margarine to the pan if necessary and stacking the crepes between waxed paper.

Note: Crepes may also be used to prepare entrées filled with creamed meat or seafood or served with a fruit sauce for dessert. Crepes freeze well in an airtight container; keep separated by the waxed paper.

Yield: 18 to 20 servings

Bread Pudding with Bourbon Sauce

1 (16-ounce) loaf French bread
1 quart skim milk
3 eggs, lightly beaten
2 cups sugar
2 tablespoons vanilla extract

1 cup raisins
1 apple, peeled, grated
3 tablespoons margarine
Bourbon Sauce (below)

Break the bread into small pieces and place in a mixing bowl. Add the milk and let stand for 10 minutes to soak.

Preheat the gas oven to 350 degrees. Stir the soaked bread until thoroughly mixed. Add the eggs, sugar, vanilla extract, raisins and apple and mix well.

Melt the margarine in a 9×13-inch baking dish. Spoon the bread mixture into the dish. Bake for 40 to 45 minutes or until firm. Let stand until cool.

Preheat the gas broiler. Cut the pudding into squares and place each in a flameproof dessert dish. Drizzle with the Bourbon Sauce and broil until bubbly.

Yield: 15 servings

Bourbon Sauce

1 cup (2 sticks) margarine, softened
2 cups sugar

2 eggs, beaten
1/4 to 1/2 cup bourbon

Cream the margarine and sugar in a mixing bowl until light and fluffy. Place in the top of a double boiler and cook over a low flame for 30 minutes or until heated through, stirring frequently.

Stir a small amount of the hot mixture into the eggs; stir the eggs into the hot mixture. Cook for 3 minutes, stirring constantly. Let stand until cool. Fold in the desired amount of bourbon.

Chocolate Decadence

1 cup (2 sticks) unsalted butter
3 (1-ounce) squares unsweetened chocolate, coarsely chopped
2 eggs, room temperature
1/4 teaspoon salt
1 cup sugar
1 tablespoon almond liqueur
1 tablespoon orange liqueur
1 teaspoon vanilla extract
1/2 cup plus 1 tablespoon flour
1/2 teaspoon baking soda
1 cup chocolate chips
1 cup chopped walnuts

Preheat the gas oven to 350 degrees. Grease an 8-inch springform pan, line the bottom with waxed paper and grease the waxed paper. Dust with a small amount of sugar and set aside.

Melt the butter and chocolate over simmering water in the top of a double boiler, stirring frequently, and set aside. Beat the eggs and salt in a bowl until thickened and lemon-colored. Add the sugar gradually, beating until pale yellow. Blend in the chocolate mixture, liqueurs and vanilla extract. Sift the flour and baking soda together into the batter and mix well. Fold in the chocolate chips and walnuts.

Pour evenly into the prepared pan. Bake for 20 to 22 minutes or until the top is firm and the center is soft. Cool in the pan on a wire rack. Place the pan on a serving plate. Loosen the Chocolate Decadence from the side of the pan with a sharp knife. Remove the side of the pan. Cut into 2-inch slices.

Yield: 8 servings

Energy Saver: Turn the thermostat on the water heater to "Low" before leaving home for a week or more.

Baked Fudge

1/2 cup sifted flour
1/2 cup baking cocoa
2 cups sugar
4 eggs, beaten

1 cup (2 sticks) margarine, melted
2 teaspoons vanilla extract
1 cup pecans

Preheat the gas oven to 350 degrees. Combine the flour, baking cocoa and sugar in a bowl and mix well. Add the eggs and mix thoroughly. Add the margarine and vanilla extract and beat well. Fold in the pecans. Spread in a greased 9×9-inch baking dish. Place the baking dish in a large baking pan.

Add 1 inch hot water to the baking pan. Bake for 1 hour or until the fudge is the consistency of custard on the bottom and crusty on top. Serve with whipped cream.

Yield: 6 to 8 servings

Baked Custard

3 cups milk
3 eggs, lightly beaten
6 tablespoons sugar

1/2 teaspoon salt
1/2 teaspoon vanilla extract
Nutmeg to taste

Preheat the gas oven to 350 degrees. Scald the milk in a medium saucepan over a medium flame. Combine the eggs, sugar, salt and vanilla extract in a bowl and mix well. Stir a small amount of the hot milk into the egg mixture; stir the egg mixture into the hot milk. Pour into ramekins or custard cups, sprinkle with nutmeg and place the ramekins in a baking pan. Add hot water to the pan to a depth level with the custard. Bake for 30 minutes or until a knife inserted in the center comes out clean. Remove the ramekins from the pan and let stand until cool. Chill until serving time.

Yield: 6 servings

Lemon Pudding Cake

1/4 cup flour
1 cup sugar
1/4 teaspoon salt
2 egg yolks, beaten

2/3 cup milk
1/4 cup fresh lemon juice
Zest of 1 lemon (about 1 teaspoon)
2 egg whites

Preheat the gas oven to 350 degrees. Sift the flour, sugar and salt together. Combine the egg yolks, milk, lemon juice and lemon zest in a large bowl and mix well. Add the dry ingredients and mix well.

Beat the egg whites in a medium bowl until stiff peaks form. Fold the egg whites into the batter. Pour into an ungreased 1-quart baking dish. Place in a large baking pan. Add 1 inch hot water to the baking pan. Bake for 50 to 55 minutes or until set and the top is well browned. Serve warm or cold with whipped cream and a garnish of additional lemon zest.

Yield: 4 to 6 servings

Rice Custard Pudding

2 cups milk
2 eggs, beaten
1/2 cup raisins
1/4 teaspoon cinnamon

1 teaspoon vanilla extract
1/2 teaspoon salt
1/2 cup sugar
1 1/4 cups cooked rice

Preheat the gas oven to 325 degrees. Scald the milk. Stir a small amount of the hot milk into the eggs; stir the eggs into the hot milk. Add the raisins, cinnamon, vanilla extract, salt, sugar and rice and mix well. Pour into a greased baking dish. Place the baking dish in a large baking pan. Add 1 inch hot water to the baking pan. Bake for 45 minutes or until the pudding is set. Remove the baking dish from the pan and let stand until cool. Chill until serving time.

Yield: 6 servings

Black Forest Squares

1 (9-ounce) package chocolate cake mix
1 cup sour cream
1 (4-ounce) package chocolate instant
   pudding mix
1 cup milk
1/4 cup crème de cassis or brandy

1 (16-ounce) can sweet pitted dark cherries
2 tablespoons sugar
1 tablespoon cornstarch
1/2 cup whipping cream
1/4 cup sliced almonds, toasted

Preheat the gas oven to 350 degrees. Prepare the cake mix using the package directions. Pour the batter into a greased and floured 9×13-inch baking pan. Bake for 10 to 12 minutes or until the cake tests done. Cool completely in the pan. Beat the sour cream, pudding mix, 1/3 cup of the milk and the crème de cassis in a mixing bowl until the mixture is fluffy. Add the remaining 2/3 cup milk gradually until the mixture is smooth. Pour over the cooled chocolate cake. Cover and chill in the refrigerator. Drain the cherries, reserving 3/4 cup syrup. Combine the sugar and cornstarch in a saucepan. Stir in the reserved syrup gradually. Cook over a medium flame until thickened and bubbly, stirring constantly. Cook for 1 minute longer, stirring constantly. Add the cherries. Remove from the flame and let stand until cool. Spread over the chilled pudding layer. Cover and chill in the refrigerator for several hours or overnight. Whip the cream to soft peaks just before serving. Pipe over the cherry layer in a lattice design. Sprinkle with the almonds. Cut into squares to serve.

Yield: 12 servings

Orange Velvet

1 (3-ounce) package orange gelatin
1/2 cup sugar
1 cup water
1 cup light corn syrup
1 cup orange juice

2 tablespoons lemon juice
2 cups milk
2 cups half-and-half
Dash of salt

Combine the gelatin and sugar in a saucepan. Stir in the water and corn syrup. Bring to a boil over a medium flame, stirring until the gelatin dissolves. Remove from the flame. Stir in the orange juice and lemon juice. Let stand and cool. Add the milk, half-and-half and salt. Pour into an ice cream freezer container. Freeze using manufacturer's directions.

Yield: 16 servings

Turkey Tips

Thawing Turkey

Thawing turkey in the refrigerator is the preferred method but it can also be thawed in cold water. Remember to keep the turkey cold while thawing. Place the turkey in the original wrap on a tray or in a pan, then into the refrigerator according to the following:

Thawing Time in the Refrigerator

Whole Turkey

8 to 12 pounds	1 to 2 days
12 to 16 pounds	2 to 3 days
16 to 20 pounds	3 to 4 days
20 to 24 pounds	4 to 5 days

Pieces of Large Turkey

half, quarter, half breast	1 to 2 days

If you forget to thaw early enough, place the turkey in a large container and cover with cold water. Change the water frequently to ensure safe and effective thawing for the necessary time needed to thaw the turkey.

Thawing Time in Cold Water

Whole Turkey

8 to 12 pounds	4 to 6 hours
12 to 16 pounds	6 to 9 hours
16 to 20 pounds	9 to 11 hours
20 to 24 pounds	11 to 12 hours

After thawing, remove the neck and giblets from the body and neck cavities. Wash the turkey inside and out. Lightly stuff the turkey allowing 3/4 cup stuffing for each pound of ready-to-cook turkey. Close the cavities with skewers, pins, clean string or toothpicks.

Roasting Turkey

Place the turkey, breast side up on a rack in a shallow roasting pan. The turkey may be brushed with melted margarine or oil, but it is not necessary. When using a meat thermometer, insert the thermometer into the thickest part of the thigh muscle without touching the bone. Cover the turkey with a lid or foil. Roast in a 325 degree gas oven according to the size of the turkey or until the thermometer registers 185 degrees. If the turkey needs additional browning, remove the cover 20 to 30 minutes before roasting is completed.

Basic Substitutions

If the recipe calls for	You can substitute:

Flour:

1 cup sifted all-purpose flour	1 cup less 2 tablespoons unsifted all-purpose flour
1 cup sifted cake flour	1 cup less 2 tablespoons sifted all-purpose flour
1 cup sifted self-rising flour	1 cup sifted all-purpose flour plus 1½ teaspoons baking powder and a pinch of salt

Milk/Cream:

1 cup buttermilk	1 cup plain yogurt, or 1 tablespoon lemon juice or vinegar plus enough milk to measure 1 cup—let stand for 5 minutes before using
1 cup whipping cream or half-and-half	⅞ cup whole milk plus 1½ tablespoons butter
1 cup light cream	⅞ cup whole milk plus 3 tablespoons butter
1 cup sour cream	1 cup plain yogurt
1 cup sour milk	1 cup plain yogurt
1 cup whole milk	1 cup skim or nonfat milk plus 2 tablespoons butter or margarine

Seasonings:

1 teaspoon allspice	½ teaspoon cinnamon plus ⅛ teaspoon cloves
1 cup ketchup	1 cup tomato sauce plus ½ cup sugar plus 2 tablespoons vinegar
1 teaspoon Italian spice	¼ teaspoon each oregano, basil, thyme, rosemary plus dash of cayenne pepper
1 teaspoon lemon juice	½ teaspoon vinegar

Sugar:

1 cup confectioners' sugar	½ cup plus 1 tablespoon granulated sugar
1 cup granulated sugar	1¾ cups confectioners' sugar, 1 cup packed light brown sugar or ¾ cup honey

Other:

1 package active dry yeast	½ cake compressed yeast
1 teaspoon baking powder	¼ teaspoon cream of tartar plus ¼ teaspoon baking soda
1 cup dry bread crumbs	¾ cup cracker crumbs or 1 cup cornflake crumbs
1 cup (2 sticks) butter	⅞ cup vegetable oil or 1 cup margarine
1 tablespoon cornstarch	2 tablespoons all-purpose flour
1 cup dark corn syrup	¾ cup light corn syrup plus ¼ cup light molasses
1 cup light corn syrup	1 cup maple syrup
1⅔ ounces semisweet chocolate	1 ounce unsweetened chocolate plus 4 teaspoons granulated sugar
1 ounce unsweetened chocolate	3 tablespoons unsweetened baking cocoa plus 1 tablespoon butter or margarine
1 (1-ounce) square chocolate	¼ cup baking cocoa plus 1 teaspoon shortening
1 cup honey	1 to 1¼ cups sugar plus ¼ cup liquid, or 1 cup corn syrup or molasses
currants	raisins
1 egg	¼ cup mayonnaise

Acknowledgments

This book came to fruition as a result of the combined efforts of ONG Home Economists who tested recipes throughout time so that delicious dishes could be prepared.

Thanks to the Corporate Communications staff who helped write and edit historical information as well as the Photographer who took rolls of film to get "the right" photo for the cover of our book. Also thanks to the Artist who reproduced drawings that were used in the early days of our recipe production.

Index

Blue Flame Favorites

A COLLECTION OF FAVORITE OKLAHOMA NATURAL GAS
RECIPES COMPILED OVER 70 YEARS

Oklahoma Natural Gas
Blue Flame Favorites
P.O. Box 401
Oklahoma City, Oklahoma 73101-0401

YOUR ORDER	QTY	TOTAL
Blue Flame Favorites at $15.95 per book		$
Shipping & handling at $3.95 for first book; $1.95 for each additional book delivered to same address		$
OK residents add 8.375% sales tax		$
TOTAL		$

Please make check payable to Oklahoma Natural Gas.

Name

Street Address

City   State   Zip

Telephone

Proceeds from the sale of this cookbook will be returned
to the communities in the ONG service territories.

Visit our website at www.ong.com.

Photocopies will be accepted.